The Irvines and Their Kin
in Nova Scotia...and Beyond
1817 – 2017

David Marshall Irvine

And

Geoffrey dePoint Irvine

Published by David Marshall Irvine in Smith's Cove, Nova Scotia

Book design, layout and formatting by Raymond Irvine.

Cover design by Raymond Irvine and Jill McLaggan.

Printed by CreateSpace, an Amazon company.

ISBN-13: 978-1548303884
ISBN-10: 1548303887

Cover illustration: *Ship TROOP* - Built at Dunbarton, Scotland, by Archibald McMillan in 1884, this was the first iron sailing ship to be owned in Canada. It is significant for us for two reasons. First because, as far as we know, it is the only Troop ship on which a member of the Irvine family, in the person of Frank Wishard Irvine (1874-1954), son of Alexander (Sandy) Irvine, sailed, at age 13, for two years as a crew member. Secondly, because it is the subject of one of the very large ships paintings, encased in beautiful gold frames, that now reside in the New Brunswick Museum, donated by A.M. Irvine, Sr., son of John Edward Irvine, who worked most of his life as a partner and part owner of the famous, east coast Troop Shipping Line.

To Sylvia, my high school sweetheart, wife and life-long best friend - finally some tangible result for the myriad hours spent in my basement hideaway on genealogical research and creating this narrative.

Acknowledgements

As I write my thanks to those who played a part in the development of this story, I realize they are mostly relatives. Still, each one deserves to be acknowledged for their individual contribution.

Fraser Stewart (4th cousin once removed) of Roger's Hill, Nova Scotia, for contacting me out of the blue some years ago and contributing the information about his 3X great grandmother and my 2nd great aunt, Margaret (Irvine) Stewart, when I visited him at his home.

Wendy Plumb of Toronto, one of only two 1st cousins on my father's side, whose assistance with the addition of her recollections of her family and our grandparents has added another dimension to this story.

Our son, Geoffrey, for his exceptionally well researched and written account of his Grandfather's military career. Thanks to him, all Dad's letters home to Mum during the war have been arranged in binders for posterity, along with a collection of pictures and other memorabilia. I hope future generations will appreciate the work he has done.

Former principal, brother John Irvine, for proofreading and providing the main content to our Mum's story from his Eulogy at her funeral.

Ray Irvine (3rd cousin), who along with his wife Jenni, now live just down the road from us in Bear River, have recently come into our lives from Manitoba, where they dabbled in publishing. Like manna from heaven, Ray has taken over my manuscript and added the pictures and captions, organized descendancy charts and generally put this manuscript into proper condition for publishing. In addition, he has taken the lead in helping me interview and ultimately select potential publishers. I could not have done it without him.

Jenni Irvine provided literary advice, along with tea and cookies as Ray and I worked at their computer.

And finally, Jill McLaggan, not a relative but our very special friend, whose advanced computer skills and artistry, fine tuned and enhanced Ray's cover design to fit the publisher's requirement.

FOREWORD

If you are reading this, you are likely a member of the Irvine family or have some close family connection. 2017 marks both the 150th anniversary of Canada's birth as a nation and the bicentenery of the arrival of our branch of the Irvine family in British North America in 1817.

You and I are the beneficiaries of years of research into the Irvine family history by David Marshall Irvine of Smith's Cove, Nova Scotia. It's only a year since I first met David, who is my 3rd cousin, and was invited to join his project as it neared completion. David generously shared his research with me and it was more than a pleasure for my wife Jenni and I to get to know David and Sylvia and to put our experience in publishing to work in bringing The Irvines and Their Kin in Nova Scotia...and Beyond to print.

Learning about my roots has been far more significant than I could have imagined three years ago when Jenni and I relocated to Nova Scotia from Manitoba. I hope that getting better acquainted with the Irvine family is as interesting an experience for you as it has been for me. Thank-you David!

Raymond Irvine
Bear River East, Nova Scotia
April 2017

For anyone interested in exploring further connections of/with the Irvine Family, there is the *David Irvine Family Tree on* Ancestry.com, containing 12,700 people, 13,500 records, 300 stories and 2,100 photos as of Sept.1, 2017. If you contact me by email at quince@eastlink.ca I can invite you to be a guest to explore the database through Ancestry.com. *DMI.*

TABLE OF CONTENTS

APPENDICES

INTRODUCTION

It is now the year 2017, which means it is 200 years since our illustrious and industrious ancestor and my 3X great grandfather, John Irvine (1763-1833) arrived by ship from Scotland to what was then part of Halifax County (Est. 1759), now Pictou County, (Est. 1835), in Nova Scotia (Est. 1625), and one of the Maritime Provinces of Canada.

Since then, Irvine descendants have scattered across Canada, the United States and in fact the world, with many remaining in the Maritime Provinces.

I was born in Cornwall, Ontario, and moved to Smith's Cove, Digby County, Nova Scotia in 1967 from Ste. Anne de Bellevue, Quebec. This year marks the 50th anniversary of that day in March 1967 when my family and I came back to where it all started and settled in Smith's Cove.

At that time, partly because my middle name is Marshall, I knew about my Marshall ancestor, Lovicia, who married my 2X great grandfather, John Irvine (1811-1849), and came from Marshalltown, about five miles from our present home in Digby County. I also knew that my father and grandfather Irvine, both of whom have middle names Marshall, had been born just across the Bay of Fundy in Saint John, New Brunswick. That was about the extent of my knowledge of my family genealogy.

Since that time, from family records and visits to archives, museums and cemeteries in Nova Scotia and New Brunswick, I have put together the following story of The Irvines and Their Kin in Nova Scotia... and Beyond. It is a story of nine generations of responsible, hard working, God fearing Irvines, all of whom contributed to the communities in which they lived and, I believe, left this world a better place.

When I set out to write this family history back in 2008, the oldest ancestor I knew about was John Irvine (1811-1849), so that was where my story originally began. Prior to that in 2002, during the genealogical research that I dabbled in for many years, I took a trip to the Dumfries area of Scotland to uncover John's past and hopefully some previously unfound generations. In preparation for my trip I contacted and joined the Dumfries and Galloway Family History Society and placed an ad in their newsletter asking for help from anyone who might also be searching for long-lost Irvines. While there I spent some time talking to their members, examining their records and visiting the local graveyards, all to no avail. Little did I know that an unknown cousin named Fraser Stewart from Pictou County, Nova Scotia, would see my ad in 2009 and contact me. Fraser is the 3X great grandson of Margaret Irvine (1792-1866), the sister of my great, great grandfather, the above-mentioned John. Although Fraser did not have much information on Margaret's and John's parents, other than that their names were John and Elizabeth, who came to Pictou County from Dumfriesshire, Scotland in 1817, he did show me the farmhouse and land they settled on and supplied considerable information about Margaret's and John's siblings and step-siblings and many of their issue.

Some years ago, to further my ability to connect with other ancestors, I had my DNA done through the auspices of the Clan Irwin Surname DNA Study. Findings as of 2017 are as follows:

- The success of this study is manifest by its steady growth over ten years to over 448 participants, so that it is now one of the 50 largest of over 8,000 surname DNA projects worldwide.

- The geographic origins in the old world of the paternal ancestry of over 85% of all participants have been ascertained. Scottish origins predominate. Some local spelling variants of the surname remain dominant within Great Britain. However, the spelling of the surname today, especially in Ireland and in the new world, has been shown to be a most unreliable indicator of the geographic origin of paternal ancestry.

- Nearly two thirds of all the Study's participants are members of a single genetic family, sharing a common ancestor who probably lived in the Scottish Borders in the 14th century[1].

- This "Borders" family includes participants representing the Irvines of Eskdale, the Irvings of Bonshaw and Dumfries (all in Dumfriesshire), the Urwins of Durham and Northumberland, and the Irvines of Castle Irvine (Co. Fermanagh, Ireland).

- Some of these participants still live in Dumfriesshire, some are descended from ancestors who migrated directly from there to North America, but the majority are descended from ancestors who probably migrated from the Borders to Ulster in the 17th century, and then from Ireland to America (typically to PA, VA, NC, SC or GA) in the 18th century, often for religious or economic reasons. This proportion of participants sharing a single common ancestor is higher than found in most other Scottish surname DNA projects.

- So far there has been only limited success in identifying genealogical relationships within our genetic families, but with only about 0.3% of the world's 100,000 adult males who today use the surname, however spelt, having undergone a Y-DNA test, this is hardly surprising. As new participants continue to join, and analysis methods improve, more relationships will be found.[2]

- The specific finding that representatives of the families of Bonshaw and Drum do not share a common paternal ancestor during the genealogical era contradicts - though does not unequivocally disprove - the tradition that the lines were related in the fourteenth century.

- These findings suggest that even within Scotland the surname has plural origins. This challenges the tradition that all Scots bearing the surname had a single ancestor.

Another more recent development has been the discovery of a family I believe to be John`s parents and siblings, who lived in Annan, not far from Dumfries in Dumfriesshire. As far as we know, none of them other than John resided in Canada, so they will not be included in this narrative other than to be listed as:

---

[1]See Appendix 1 for information on "The Border Reivers", including the Irvines

[2] Many historical articles have been written about the Irvines, including the one found in Appendix 2

William Irvine (1738) and Harriet Thompson (abt. 1742), and children John (1763), Janet (1765), William (1767), George (1770), Jean (1774), Margaret (1774) and Thomas (1776).

Regarding ancestors, it should be mentioned that although our founding Marshall ancestors were pre-Loyalist New England Planters and our Irvines came directly from Scotland, we owe our beginnings in Canada predominantly to the staunch United Empire Loyalists belonging to the White, Roop, Wright, Craibe, Dykeman and Hatfield families. In addition, William White (1577-1621), my 9th great grandfather, came to the United States on the *MAYFLOWER*.

If you visit England or Scotland, Irvine is inevitably pronounced "Irvin," which our family has always attempted to do with little success in Canada and especially in the Maritimes where "Irving" is a well-known name. Getting the name pronounced correctly is even more difficult in the United States, where there is a large city in California named Irvine, but pronounced with a vine, as in wine.

Throughout this narrative, you will find various descendancy charts covering the Irvine Family by generation beginning with John and Elizabeth to better clarify who is who and where they fit in the family starting with John as the first generation known to have lived in Canada. Then in Appendix 18, you will find more detailed Descendancy Charts for the three sons of the second-generation John Irvine.

To clarify the connection with previous generations, you will find the line of progression in brackets from the first John, who came to Nova Scotia in 1817. For example, after my name in the 6th generation, appears (*John, John, John, Arthur Marshall, Arthur Marshall*).

FIRST GENERATION

John Irvine (1763- 1833)

My story of the Irvines in Canada begins with John and Elizabeth and their eight children who came to Pictou County by ship from Scotland sometime between 1817 and 1822. There is some indication of an Irish connection, since the crest on the ring that Dad's grandmother (Julia Elvira (White) Irvine) gave him and which he wore all his life, appears to have been of Irish origin. Unfortunately, we will never know for sure since many parish records from that period have been lost and during that period there was a great deal of travel back and forth between the Dumfriesshire area of Scotland and Ireland.

Dad's first cousin, the Rt. Hon. Sir Bryant Godman-Irvine, a Member of the British Parliament, had the same crest that was given to him by the same Grandmother Irvine. When he checked it with Lord Lyon, King of Arms of Great Britain, the report was as follows:

> This appears to be the crest of arms confirmed to Lieutenant Colonel Gerard Irvine of Castle Fartagh on 1st September 1673, who died after all his three sons and is reported to not have any other direct descendant. He did have a younger brother, William, who might have carried on the line and the crest. The heraldic description of the crest is: 'Argent a fess gules between three holly leaves vert`, with the motto - 'Dum memor ipse mei ', probably meaning 'Faithful unto death'. This branch of the Irvines was from the Bonshaw family.

Further, the Genealogist of the Irish Chief Herald wrote: "the crest would seem to suggest a link with the Irvines of Rochfield (and surrounding town lands), County Fermanagh, Ireland."

Then Burke's *Landed Gentry of Ireland* includes: "The Irvines of Castle Irvine are of very ancient Scottish ancestry. They are directly descended from the Irvines of Bonshaw, County Dumfries, the first of the name on record being Robert de Herewine, A.D. 1226. The family seat is Castle Irvine, Irvinestown, Ireland."[3]

Although it appears that we developed from the Bonshaw line, we really do not know whether we are of Drum or Bonshaw, so thus I have included all available crests in the Appendices.[4] They are not Coats of Arms of any one person, but rather somewhat generic representations of Irvine and associated clans. The common thread throughout all of them is the holly leaf.

To get back to John`s arrival, we have learned that the two vessels *HOPE* and *WILLIAM TELL* landed passengers at Sydney, Nova Sotia on 23rd and 25th July 1817 respectively. We are told in a secondary source that "in 1817 the ship *WILLIAM TELL*, came out to Canso, Nova Scotia with settlers from Barra". The petition informs us that most passengers on their ship remained on Cape Breton Island.

---

[3] See Appendix 3 for information on the Irvines of Castle Irvine, which we visited a few years ago on a trip to Ireland.

[4] See Appendix 4 for illustrations of Irvine family crests

Further, in the summer of 1817 a party of newly-landed Scots immigrants put in a petition to the Nova Scotia government for relief and assistance. Thirty-four Scots signed this document, and thirty-three of them seem to have traveled on the same vessel. The petition of date July 31, 1817, gives information concerning ninety-four arrivals in Pictou on that day, apparently in dreadful circumstances.

In the case of a signatory to the petition, corroborating evidence seems to have been found. In 1818 one Murdock Gillis from the Island of Barra sought a grant of land. He mentions that he had arrived in 1817 in Nova Scotia. A man of the same name was a petitioner in the document of 1817. Likewise, both documents have Roderick Gillis with wife and six children and arriving in Pictou in 1817.

If all these pieces fit, it seems to be that the *WILLIAM TELL*, out of Greenock, Scotland, landed most of its passengers at Sydney, on Cape Breton Island, and then came through the Gut of Canso to land the remainder of its human cargo at Pictou six days later. Included in the list of petitioners was a John Irvine, who appeared to be alone as no wife or children were listed after his name, unlike many others.

Although the account indicates that some of the immigrants were from the Island of Barra, there is no reason to assume that all, including John Irvine were also. Annan, in Dumfriesshire, where John was supposed to originate, is relatively close to Greenock.

The first indication we have of the Irvine's arrival in Pictou County is found in county land records, which show the purchase of two hundred acres of land from George Smith at Roger's Hill, Pictou County in 1822. That property is just down the road from Fraser Stewart's home. We do not know if John's wife Elizabeth died before or after they arrived in Nova Scotia, but we do know that all her children with John, namely **Margaret (1792-1866), William**

John Irvine Farm at Roger's Hill

(1795-1870), Isabella (1800?), Ann (1804-1847), Hugh (1807-1880), John (1811-1849), Joseph (1815) and Jean (?) were born in Scotland. Although we do not know Elizabeth's maiden surname, there is a hint that it may have been "Mair", since the only son with a middle name is Hugh Mair Irvine. Because John's will does not mention Jean, we can assume she died at an early age between 1816 and 1833. Although we know that John was a farmer after he arrived in Canada, we know nothing about his activities prior to his arrival. John died in 1833 and his will states his body was to be interred in the West River Churchyard. No death certificate or gravestone have yet been found to corroborate this fact. When Fraser Stewart and I searched the Durham Churchyard we found only Margaret's grave, marked with a very substantial obelisk.

John IRVINE (b. 1763-D, Scotland d. 26 Mar 1833-RsH, PC, NS)

sp: Elizabeth ?? (b. 1800-Dumfrieshire, Scotland)

— Margaret IRVINE (b. 1792-Dumfriesshire, Scotland d. 14 Dec 1866-Roger's Hill, PC, NS)

  sp: Robert STEWART (b. 1795-D, Scotland d. 3 Jun 1883-Roger's Hill, PC, NS)

— William IRVINE (b. 1795-Dumfries Shire, Scotland d. 1 Nov 1870-Barney`s River, NS)

  sp: Janet RAE (b. 1795-Dumfries Shire, Scotland d. 16 May 1875-BsR, PC, NS)

— Isabella IRVINE (b. 1800-Scotland d. ?)

  sp: George RAE (b. 1797 d. 1852)

— Ann IRVINE (b. 1804-Scotland d. 1847)

  sp: Robert MACLELLAN (b. 1797 d. 1874)

— Hugh Mair IRVINE (b. 1807-Dumfrieshire, Scotland d. 5 Aug 1880-BOQ, C, C, Australia)

  sp: Anna Maria CLAWSON (b. 1812-SJ, NB m. 23 Mar 1849 d. 14 Aug 1882-, , , Aus)

— John IRVINE (b. 4 Jun 1811-Dumfries, Scotland d. 25 Oct 1849-Quebec City, P.Q.)

  sp: Lovicia Ellen (Lavicy) MARSHALL (b. 20 Jun 1815-, m. 1840 ?? d. 17 Jun 1898-)

— Joseph IRVINE (b. 1815-Dumfries, Scotland)

  sp: Mary Jane WHOOTEN (b. 1824)

— Jean IRVINE (b. Unknown-Scotland)

Jean (Jane) (Murray) Irvine (second wife)

After Elizabeth's death, perhaps in early 1820, John married Jean (Jane) Murray in 1824 or '25 and they had five more children: **Andrew (1826), Christy Ann (1828), Elizabeth (1829), Alexander (1831- 1915) and another Margaret (1833)**. Jane was pregnant with Margaret at the time of John's death. Jane was born about 1800 in Aberdeen or Inverness, Scotland and died in 1883. Her mother was Christina Sutherland.

Jane Irvine and her family left Roger's Hill in the early 1850s and moved to the United States. For some unknown reason, Jane and all her family and their descendants changed their last name to "Irving". Her sons, who as young men worked at the shipyards in Pictou, worked in the shipyards at Bath, Maine, then at Mobile and Savannah, where Andrew died. They finally settled in Mystic, Conn., where Jane, two of the three daughters and Alexander lived out the remainder of their lives. Helen Grant Irving, a daughter of Alexander's, married Carl Cutler and lived and died in Mystic, Conn.

6

Descendents of John Irvine from Second Wife Jean Murray

2   sp: Jean (Jane) MURRAY

Andrew IRVINE (b.1826)

    sp: Madeline UNKNOWN

Christiana (Christy) Ann IRVINE (b.1828)

    sp: Angus MACDONALD (b.Abt 1851)

Elizabeth IRVINE (b.1829 d.1919)

    sp: Findlay CAMPBELL

    sp: Enoch SHORE

Alexander IRVINE (b.1831 d.1915)

    sp: Hannah Gore PARKER (b.1840 m.1878)

Margaret J. IRVINE (b.1833)

    sp: Benjamin LAMPHERE

SECOND GENERATION

Margaret Irvine (1792-1866) *(John)*

Perhaps Margaret and Robert Stewart were married in Scotland for they immigrated together to Nova Scotia in 1817, several years before the rest of Margaret's siblings. Margaret would have been 25 at the time. Robert applied for a land grant in 1820 and was granted 200 acres of land in Barney's River, Pictou County, Nova Scotia in 1828. By John's will, Robert then acquired Margaret's brother, William's, share of an additional 50 acres. In 1839, he sold the 250 acres to William and then in 1843 he purchased brother-in-law Hugh's share of 50 acres, so all his holdings were concentrated at Roger's Hill. As a wheelwright, it is understood that Robert made spinning wheels.

Margaret's obituary on the 3rd of January 1867 read, "At Roger's Hill, Dec. 14, Margaret Irvine, the beloved wife of Robert Stewart, Elder, in the 74th year of her age. The deceased was a native of Dumfriesshire, Scotland, emigrated to this country in 1817. For a period upwards of 50 years she was a consistent member of the Presbyterian Church, displaying during life the meek and quiet disposition of her Savior, and during a protracted illness, the most cheerful submission to the Divine Will."

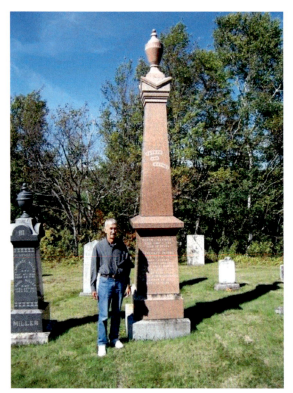

Margaret Irvine's gravestone with Fraser Stewart

Then some years later, the *Pictou County Eastern Chronicle* of 21 June 1883 reported, "At Roger's Hill, Mr. Robert Stewart, Elder, aged 88 years, deceased on the 3rd inst. He was a native of Dumfriesshire, Scotland, but has for many years resided in this Country and was widely known as an intelligent member of society and an active zealous church worker. He long filled the office of Elder in the congregation of the West River under successive pastors, who all found him a faithful supporter in every good work, while the congregation had much reason to value his self-denying efforts on their behalf as long as strength was continued."

I will mention Margaret and Robert's son, John Stewart here because in 1841 at the age of 20 he left his home at Roger's Hill and moved to Saint John to work for his uncles John and Hugh Irvine. Upon his death at age 79, during a tribute from the Session of St. David's Church, Saint John, he was described as follows: "His splendid genius and quick perception soon won for him the promotion his abilities and correct habits so richly deserved. Faithful in that which is least, he rose step by step in all the stages of his chosen profession, until he had become one of the leading shipbuilders and shipowners in the Maritime Provinces."

William Irvine (1795-1879) *(John)*

We know very little about William except that it appears he came first to Rogers's Hill, then moved to Barney's River and farmed the 250 acres purchased from Robert Stewart in 1839. According to Fraser Stewart, no Irvines remain on that land today.

The Pictou *Presbyterian Witness* indicates William died 1 November 1879 at Upper Settlement, Barney's River, having emigrated in 1820 from Annan, Dumfriesshire, Scotland. This is really the only indication we have that the family came from Annan, although to complicate matters, in the ledger of the Clandish Free Presbyterian Church, Barney's River, William is listed as coming from Kirkpatrick Flemming, which is five miles from Annan!

Isabella Irvine (1800- ?) *(John)*

Ann Irvine (1804-1847) *(John)*

Hugh Mair Irvine (1807-1880) *(John)*

Along with his brothers, John and Joseph, Hugh left Barney's River and moved to Saint John, New Brunswick, sometime in the mid 1830s. We can presume they acquired their ship building skills in the Pictou shipyards, but we do know they launched their first ship, the *EDINA*, a 471-ton barque in July 1839. From then until 1850, Hugh and his brothers, or Hugh alone, built 15 more ships ranging in size from a 113-ton schooner to the last ship built by Hugh alone, the *OTTILLIA*, a 923-tonner registered in Saint John in May 1850 with Hugh Irvine listed as builder, owner and master (William Irvine was later appointed as master).[5] Hugh is listed in Poll Books for the City of Saint John 1842-53 as residing in King's Ward in 1848. By January 1851 Hugh Irvine, shipwright, late of Saint John, now of Liverpool, England was registering the *OTTILLIA*, which he sold in 1852.

Hugh Irvine apparently caught the Australian fever in Liverpool, when news came of the discovery of gold. He and his family returned to Saint John and one of the Saint John papers reported in September 1852, that Hugh Irvine; his wife, Ann Maria (Clawson)Irvine, and their daughter Mary Eliza (aged 2), along with 2 children, Emma Bonner (1837) and William Bonner (1839), from Anna Maria's first marriage, had sailed on the barque *AMELIA* for Port Philip (Melbourne), Australia.

The following is an account by one of Hugh and Anna Irvine's shipmates:

> In 1852 I sailed from St. John in the bark "Amelia", under the command of Capt. HOLDER of Westfield, for the gold fields of Australia. There were 48 of us all told in the vessel, Hugh Irvine, the ship builder and his family being among the number. We were just 100 days on the voyage from St. John to a bay near Melbourne and never dropped anchor all that time. It was a day before Christmas we made our final soundings. Once on land we started for the

---

[5] See Appendix 5 for list of ships built by various of the Irvine brothers.

diggings. Carts and horses were needed for the journey before us, our objective point being the Ovens Diggings on the Ovens river, 230 miles distant from Melbourne. Mr. Shanks from Indiantown (St. John) got us carts and horses and we set out on our journey. Forty miles from Melbourne two of our horses were stolen one night and we were thus left in a bad way, as every horse had its load to draw and there was not a pound of weight of stuff that we could afford to throw away. Fortunately for us the police magistrate at Kilmorie, where the theft occurred, was a son of Rev. Coster of Carleton, St. John, and he interested himself in our behalf so effectually that the animals were speedily found. So was the thief. As the driver who owned the horses was an old convict and the thief was ditto, no time was wasted in going to law. They settled the case on the spot. One man was alive at the end of the battle. So were his horses. And we moved on. We were 17 days on the journey. Once at the mines we all fell to and I dug awhile. Everybody delves for gold when he first reaches the place where it is known to lie waiting, it may be for thousands of years to be turned up to the light of the sun.

Once in Australia they appear to have changed their name to Irving and produced three more children- John Irving (1853-1863) and twins- Eva Marion Irving (1859-1863) and Ida Amelia Irving (1859-1901). John and Eva died 12 days apart of diphtheria when the family was on the gold fields and are listed together on the death certificate.

The family moved to Queenscliff, at the mouth of Port Phillip Bay, that has a fishing industry and boat yards and Hugh became once again a boat builder.

In 1862 Hugh is listed as Honorary Secretary of the Wesleyan Church in Campbell's Reef and in 1868 he was the Reservoir Keeper at Moyston. Also, in the late 1860s, there is an indication that Hugh took up with a radical religious fanatic named John Simons Stephens and was his main deputy in the sect called the "New Lights". In 1873 Hugh gave Notice of Sale at Moyston.

Hugh died of asthma and bronchitis at the age of 73 on Mercer Street in the Burough of Queenscliff, County of Grant, Australia, on 4 August 1880. Anna Marie died 13 August 1882 at Geelong, GrantCounty, Victoria, Australia.

The oldest daughter Mary Eliza married John Stephens and they moved into the country, but returned to Queenscliff later. They had 6 children and one of them Ethel Ida Rosebella Virginia Stephens was delivered by Mary's sister Ida Amelia Irving in a railway signal box at Mangalore in Victoria. Ethel ended up marrying one of Ida Amelia' step sons George Bartholomew Jeffery, from her husbands 2nd marriage, so connected to the Jeffery family twice. Ida Amelia Irving married Walter De Molesworth Jeffery on 15th May 1888 and had 6 children.

John Irvine (1811-1849) *(John)*

According to John's gravestone, he was born in Dumfries, Scotland on June 11th, 1811. John died of cholera on board the ship *IOWA* in Quebec City on October 25th, 1849. His funeral was in St. Andrews Presbyterian Church, Quebec City and he was buried in St. Mathews Cemetery in Quebec City.

John Irvine's grave - Quebec City

We know from letters John wrote to his wife from Liverpool in July and August of 1849, that he had delivered the ship *IOWA,* which he and his brother Hugh had built, to be sold in Liverpool.[6] The final letter dated October 5[th,] was posted after arriving back in Quebec City (Quebeck) on his way home to Saint John on board the *IOWA* that was carrying cargo for the new owners. John never made it back to his home port and his family, but died of cholera just twenty days after posting the letter. No doubt he contracted the disease in Liverpool, where 5,308 persons died of the dreaded disease in 1849 during a worldwide pandemic.

The following appeared in the Saint John, New Brunswick *Morning News* on November 2nd, 1849: "We regret to learn that Mr. John Irvine, shipbuilder of this city, died at Quebec on the 25th wit., after a short sickness. He had proceeded to Quebec on the ship *Iowa*, and while there was seized with a sickness which terminated fatally. Mr. Irvine has left a wife and family and a large circle of friends in this city, to mourn their loss."

John's Last Will and Testament, dated May 25th, 1849, names as his executors Hugh Irvine, his brother, and Charles Duff, his lawyer. The will states, in part: "And I do hereby declare that the said Trustees and the survivor of them shall stand seised and possessed of all my real estate, and of the said mortgage securities. Upon trust to pay over, out of the clear annual rents, profits, interest and income thereof, to my wife Lavicy Ellen, the sum of Forty pounds, per annum, so long as she shall remain unmarried, and if the said yearly income shall exceed the sum of forty pounds, then to expend the surplus, in such manner as shall appear most judicious to the Trustees, or the survivor of them, in the education and maintainance of my children;" Note the old spelling of "seized" and "maintenance ".

The will was probated in Saint John on November 12th, 1849 and the probate document indicates: "that he died seised of or otherwise entitled unto personal estate to the value of Five Hundred pounds." Other documents prepared for the Surrogate Court are dated August 24th, 1853 and appear to indicate the final

---

[6] See Appendix 6 for the four letters John wrote to his wife, Lovicia.

distribution of funds from the partnership between Hugh and John, leaving John's heirs with a grand total of 53 pounds, 12 shillings and 7 pence!

Unfortunately, because John died at the early age of 38, and appeared to be busy building ships throughout his time in Canada, we have very little information about him. We do know that in 1849 he was a Member of The St. Andrews Society of Saint John, since their membership list from 1798 to 1903 carries his name. I have in my possession two St. Andrews Society medals (one is sterling silver) that would have belonged to John and maybe also to his son John Edward, who was later a member of record in 1890.[7]

In addition to Hugh (1809-1880), with whom John was in business building ships (including the *IOWA*), there may have been other brothers including Joseph, who first accompanied them to Saint John. Chapter 13 in Saint John Ships and Their Builders is titled "Hugh Irvine and Brothers ". In the letters John wrote to his wife, while in Liverpool in 1849, he refers to a Thomas Irvine and there is a reference in the above-mentioned Chapter 13 to a William Irvine as being the Master of the *OTTILLIA*, the last ship Hugh built in 1850, after John's death. Since he sends "his respect" to Thomas Irvine in the letters, it is possible that Thomas was an older relative.

We do know that John was living in Saint John in July 1839 when he and Hugh completed and launched the 471-ton barque, *EDINA*. Very shortly thereafter the following account appeared in a supplement to the *Saint John Courier* on August 19th, 1839:

> AWFUL CONFLAGRATION - One Hundred Buildings Destroyed
>
> We have the melancholy task of announcing another awful visitation to St. John- the destruction by fire of a large portion of the City, including about fifty extensive mercantile establishments. The fire was discovered a few minutes before nine o'clock on Saturday night, August 17th, bursting from a house on Nelson Street, owned by C & B Lawton, occupied as a store and warehouse by Messrs. Hugh Irvine and Brothers, ship-builders, and the upper part as dwellings, which continued burning until daylight yesterday morning before its devouring progress was stayed.

It goes on to itemize all the buildings that were lost, then continues:

> So intense was the heat that the buildings on the South Market Wharf were frequently on fire, although separated from those on the North by a Slip of one hundred and fifty feet, and a roadway on each wharf of twenty-five feet, making in all a distance of two hundred feet.
>
> The rigging of several small vessels lying in the Slip (it being low water at the time), having ignited, it became necessary to cut away their masts to save them from entire destruction, and to prevent the communication of the flames to the opposite side of the Slip. The American schooner *COMPEER*, lying at the South Market Wharf, was among the number.

---

[7] See Appendix 7 for examples of St Andrews medals

We are glad to hear that notwithstanding the great confusion which prevailed, no human lives are known to be lost, several persons, however, received severe bruises.

The fire is said to have had its origin in the flame of a candle coming in contact with oakum lying upon a cask of brandy, from which a lad was drawing some of the liquor in the premises occupied by the Messrs. Irvine. The total amount of property destroyed, including buildings, merchandise and household effects, cannot fall far short of 200,000. Pounds.

Lovicia Ellen Marshall

Since neither of the Irvine brothers had children at that point in time, we can presume that the space over the warehouse was being occupied by someone other than either of the Irvine Brothers.

The result of the fire and a subsequent larger fire in 1877, was that Saint John has the largest and richest collection of turn-of-the-century architecture in all of Canada, including many of the houses that were owned by our ancestors.

Between 1838, when that first ship would have been started, and 1841, when their first son was born, John married Lovicia Ellen Marshall, (also called Lavicy/Levicy – John 's will refers to her as Lavicy Ellen, the name on her gravestone is Leovicy E. I will call her Lovicia, the name that appears most often), of Marshalltown, Digby County, Nova Scotia. Lovicia was born in Marshalltown in 1816 or 17 and was the daughter of Solomon Marshall (1779-1831) and Martha (Patty) Inglis (1784-1864). Solomon was born in 1779 in Marshalltown, the son of Anthony James Marshall (1728-1839) after whom Marshalltown was named.[8]

Marshalltown was originally called Birchtown, but changed after Anthony moved there in either 1760 or 1761. Anthony, who was born 1738 in Billerica, Middlesex County, Massachusetts was one of four brothers who were Planters that settled first in Granville Ferry, Annapolis County in 1758 or 1759. Anthony moved to Birchtown while the other three moved a short distance to Wilmot. Martha Inglis was born in 1784 in Glasgow, Scotland and died in Marshalltown on February 3rd, 1864. Martha and Solomon were married May 13, 1802.

Solomon was one of nine passengers on the Digby-Saint John packet schooner, *CAROLINE* driven off course and wrecked on Isle au Haute with loss of all passengers and crew on December 18th,1831. He is buried in St. Paul's Church Cemetery, Marshalltown, along with Anthony and Martha and many other related Marshalls.[9]

---

[8] See New England Planters of Annapolis County, Anthony Marshall, Louella Marshall and genealogy on bros Isaac, William and Solomon Marshall, Louella A. (Hicks) Marshall and Ina V. (Marshall) Oliver, Annapolis Heritage Soc., ISBN 978-0-9784586-8-3
[9] See Isiah Wilson's History of Digby County, pages 162-165 for a poem recounting the loss of the Packet CAROLINE.

After Solomon's early death, Martha married Solomon's brother, Richard, whose first wife, Hannah Bacon (1774- 1850) had died. Martha and Richard were married on October 14th, 1852.

John and Lovicia had three sons, all born in Saint John: **Alexander (Sandy) was born in 1841, Hugh Marshall was born November 6th, 1843 and John Edward was born December 29th, 1846**.

After John died, Lovicia returned to Marshalltown, Nova Scotia, where she resided while the boys were very young, however, on August 25th, 1857 she married Alfred Troop (1816-1875) and moved to Granville Ferry. Alfred was the brother of Jacob Valentine Troop, M.P.P., founder of the famous Troop Line of sailing ships. Alfred and Lovicia are buried in the Mills Family Cemetery in Granville Ferry because Alfred was previously married to Sarah Ann Mills (1821-1856).

Since Hugh and John built a number of ships for the Troops, it is reasonable to assume that the families would have been acquainted with each other in Saint John.

Lovicia (Irvine) Troop's Gravestone

Alfred Troop's Gravestone

Joseph Irvine (1815 -?) *(John) (1st wife)*
Jean Irvine (? - ?) *(1st wife)*
Andrew Irvine (1826- ?) *(John) (2nd wife)*
Christiana (Christy) Ann Irvine (1828 -?) *(John) (2nd wife)*
Elizabeth Irvine (1829 – 1919) *(John) (2nd wife)*

Alexander Irvine (1831-1915) *(John) (2ⁿᵈ wife)*

Alexander's obituary in the *Norwich Bulletin* reads as follows:

> Alexander Irving died at his home at West Mystic Sunday afternoon after a long illness from rheumatism. Although he had been in failing health his death came as a shock to his relatives and friends. Mr. Irving was one of the last Mystic shipbuilders and was born in Pictou, N.S., July 18, 1831, the son of John and Jane Irving, who were natives of Dumfriesshire, Scotland. In his boyhood days, he worked in the shipyards of his native town and became a ship carpenter. Afterward he went to Savanah, GA., where his brother (Andrew) had charge of a large drydock. Here he stayed until he was called to Mobile, AL. to assist in the construction of the largest steamer ever built on the Mississippi River.

> From there he went to Bath, ME., and in 1861 went to work at Norwich, CT., to take charge of the work on government gunboats. In July of that years he came to Mystic and assisted in the building of the gunboat ONASCO. He laid the stem and the stern of the ironclad GALENA, the first ironclad ever constructed in the United States, and built several gunboats for the Cuban government.

> After the civil war, he built the ship DAUNTLESS for the late Charles P. Williams of Stonington, and in the 70s was a member of the shipbuilding firm of Maxon & Irving of West Mystic. Under his direction many barges and tugboats were constructed for the Thames Towboat Company. The schooners DONNA T. BRIGGS and GRACE F. WILLARD were built under his supervision. Mr. Irving has always been known as a master shipbuilder and was especially liked by the men in his employ, for the reason he never asked them to do anything he could not do himself.

> He was a Knight Templar and for many years was a master of Mystic Council, R. and S. M. He was united in marriage on December 31ˢᵗ, 1877 with Miss Hannah Gore Packer, who survives him, with two sons, John Irving of Poquonnoc and George P. Irving of West Mystic, and one daughter, Mrs. Carl Cutler of Fort George, B.C., and a sister Mrs. Elizabeth Shore of Meadville, MO.

Margaret J. Irvine (1833-?) *(John) (2ⁿᵈ wife)*

Descendants of John IRVINE

1st	2nd

John IRVINE (b.1811 d.1849)

   sp: Lovicia Ellen MARSHALL (b.1815 m.1840 d.1898) ———— Alexander (Sandy) IRVINE (b.1841 d.1911)

                                                            sp: Mary E. PIGGOTT (b.1847 m.1864 d.1919)

                                     Hugh Marshall IRVINE (b.1843 d.1913)

                                                             sp: Martha Ann MILLS (b.1843 m.1867 d.1922)

                                     John Edward IRVINE (b.1846 d.1911)

                                                               sp: Julia Elvira WHITE (b.1852 m.1874 d.1938)

THIRD GENERATION

Alexander (Sandy) Irvine (1841-1911) *(John, John)*

Alexander Irvine's Gravestone

At some point Alexander moved to the United States, where he died in Providence, Rhode Island on September 12th, 1911. He married Mary Piggott (1847-1919) and they had four children: **Lillian (1866-1924), Frank (1874-1954), Eva (1876-1957) and Violet (1880-1945)**. I do not have any information on Lillian, Eva or Violet, but Frank's story as follows under 4th generation is quite interesting. Alexander is buried in the Mills Cemetery in Granville Ferry, with his mother.

Descendants of Alexander (Sandy) IRVINE

1st	2nd
Alexander (Sandy) IRVINE (b.1841 d.1911)	
sp: Mary E. PIGGOTT (b.1847 m.1864 d.1919)	Lillian IRVINE (b.1865 d.1924)
	sp: Frank B / MORGAN (b.Abt 1862 m.1893)
	Frank Wishard IRVINE (b.1874 d.1954)
	sp: P SCHROEDER (b.1879 m.1903 d.1956)
	Eva Estelle / IRVINE (b.1876 d.1957)
	sp: Alfred W D PETT D (b.1869 m.1903 d.19
	Violet Ethel IRVINE (b.1878 d.1945)
	sp: Charles A TUTTLE (b.1886 m.1909 d.195

Hugh Marshall Irvine (1843-1913) *(John, John)*

John's son, Hugh, married Martha Ann Mills (1843-1922) of Granville Ferry on November 6th, 1867 in Granville Ferry. Hugh was at one time, Postmaster at Granville Ferry, N.S. and for some years was associated in business with his half brother, Alfred Troop, in the general store known as "Troop and Irvine".

The *Annapolis Spectator* of Thursday, July 17, 1913 carried the following that appeared originally in the *Morning Chronicle* of July 16th, "There passed away on Saturday morning, one of Granville Ferry's most respected citizens, in the person of Hugh M. Irvine, aged 69 years. The deceased had been a Justice of the Peace for a long period of years, and Postmaster at Granville Ferry for 38 years as well as keeping a general store. He was the son of John Irvine of St John. A widow and 3 sons survive him. Mrs Irvine is a daughter of the late David Mills, and the sons are John A., William and Alton D., all in the west. The funeral was today."

Hugh Marshall Irvine

Some years later in 1922, the *Granville Ferry News* indicated that: "Mrs Martha Mills Irvine, widow of Hugh M Irvine, (for many years postmaster in this village), passed away at the home of her sister, Mrs John Bent, in Belleisle on May 5th, aged 79 years. The funeral was today."

The gravestone in Stoney Beach Cemetery indicates Hugh's death as July 1st, 1913 and Martha's as May 4th, 1922.

Martha and Hugh had three sons, **John Alfred (1868-1928), William Andrew (1870-1940) and Alton David (1874-1956).**

Hugh Irvine and Family

Hugh Marshall and Margaret Irvine's Gravestone

Descendants of Hugh Marshall IRVINE

1st   2nd

Hugh Marshall IRVINE (b.1843 d.1913)

  sp: Martha A MILLS (b.1843 m.1867 d.1922)   John Alfred IRVINE (b.1868 d.1928)

                                   sp: Mina C BUCKLEY (b.1879 m.1901 d.1967

                           William Andrew IRVINE (b.1870 d.1940)

                                   sp: Jane Wallace PIGGOTT (b.1872 d.1941)

                           Alton David IRVINE (b.1874 d.1956)

                                   sp: A M ROBERTSON (b.1882 m.1904 d.196(

John Edward Irvine (1846-1911) *(John, John)*

John Edward Irvine

Of greatest interest to me is John and Lovicia`s youngest son, my great grandfather, John Edward (1846-1911), who was born in Saint John; moved to Marshalltown; then to Granville Ferry; and in 1861 he returned to Saint John.

In 1866, he entered the employ of Troop and Sons, who in the days of wooden vessels operated the largest shipping firm in eastern Canada. In 1881, he was received into partnership and remained at the firm till 1905. An interesting note hand-written by someone in the margin of a newspaper clipping about the Troop Shipping Line and Family states: "This does not mention J. E. Irvine, who really kept the Troop's heads above water a good many years when they were sadly floundering."

Newspaper reports at the time of his death refer to him as, "a Man who was for many years one of Saint John's most highly respected citizens." Reference is made to his ardent work in Centenary Queen's Square Methodist Church, the St. Andrew's Society and as being one of the leading spirits in the YMCA.

J E Irvine Family L to R- Nell, Harry, John E., Edna, Arthur and Julia

John E. Irvine is described in a letter from Arthur M. Gregg, General Secretary of the YMCA in Saint John, to Grandpa Irvine in 1946 as follows: "No person did more to bring into being the YMCA in this City than your Father, the late John E. Irvine and I would hope in the proposed New Building his name may be memorialized in some suitable way. Few families in Saint John have given greater leadership to this movement throughout the years. The older men have always told me that it was your Father's influence more than any other that brought the organization about and that although he was not the first president this honour could have been his, if he had not desired to press other men into that position.

As President from 1883 to 1887 he established a record that has never been equalled in years of service by any other person occupying the President's office."

At various times John E. was connected with boards of management of the Boy's Industrial Home, the Protestant Orphan's Home and the Home for the Incurables. He was also a regent of Mount Allison University.[10]

Julia Elvira (White) Irvine

On October 16, 1874 John married Julia Elvira White (1852-1938) in Saint John. Julia was the daughter of William Henry White (1820-1901) and his second wife Eliza Jane Hatfield (1830-1886), both from prominent New Brunswick Loyalist Families. [11]

Julia and John had five children - **Mary Edna (1875-1963), William Henry (1878-1957), Arthur Marshall (1881-1952), Kenneth Ingles (1883- lived for 10 days), and Helen (Nell) S. (1886-1980)**.

In 1906 John and Julia moved to Calgary, where John entered business with the Mutual Life Assurance Company of Canada with his son, William Henry. He also took a large interest in the lives of the people by becoming a member of the executive of the YMCA and first President of the Alberta Bible Society. He was also a director of the Board of Trade and a member of the Canadian Club. It was reported that the Central Methodist Church, with its great membership and well-organized institutions, found in him a deeply interested and efficient worker.

[10] See Appendix 8 for newspaper clipping about John Edward Irvine

[11] See Appendix 9 re: exerpts from *History of the White Family,* pages 28 and 29 concerning Elvira's father William Henry White

28 Garden Street – John and Julia on the front steps of their home

Descendants of John Edward IRVINE

1st   2nd

John Edward IRVINE (b.1846 d.1911)

   sp: Julia E WHITE (b.1852 m.1874 d.1938)   Mary Edna IRVINE (b.1875 d.1963)

                                    sp: J E C ANGEVINE (b.1873 m.1900 d.1936)

                       William Henry (Harry) IRVINE (b.1878 d.1957

                                      sp: Martha UNKNOWN (b.1873)

                                      sp: Ada Mary BRYANT (b.1873)

                       Arthur Marshall IRVINE Sr. (b.1881 d.1952)

                                      sp: Lulah L CRAIBE (b.1881 m.1905 d.1957)

                       Kenneth Inglis IRVINE (b.1883 d.1883)

                       Helen Stuart "Nell" IRVINE (b.1886 d.1980)

                                      sp: K R SCHOFIELD (b.1885 m.1912 d.1962)

FOURTH GENERATION

Lillian Irvine (1866-1924) *(John, John, Alexander)*

Frank Wishard Irvine (1874-1954) *(John, John, Alexander)*

Frank Wishard Irvine was born in Yarmouth, Nova Scotia, on August 27th, 1874. In a letter written to Grandpa Irvine (AMI Sr.) Frank explains that from 1887 to 1889 he sailed on the Troop Line ship *TROOP* out of Saint John and says, "some of the happiest days of my life was spent on her" and adds that "other Irvines were going to sea in 1770". Among Grandpa Irvine's collection of large ship paintings, was one of the ship *TROOP,* which is pictured on the cover.

From a form he signed when he applied for a passport on December 11th, 1922, we learn that in 1889 he sailed from Annapolis Royal and lived for the next 31 years in Boston and New York. He became a US naturalized citizen in Boston, Mass. on January 6th, 1896, at which time he was a Master Mariner and lived at 661 Westminster Road in Brooklyn, New York. On the passport application Captain Irvine indicates that he plans to sail from New York to England on the S/S *AMERICA* on December 14th, 1922 at 10 am and be away for two months.

According to information that someone in the past received from an A. Irvine Pett of Cuyahoga Falls, Ohio in September of 1958, Frank Irvine was at one time the youngest captain of steam to sail from New York Harbour. He was commander of a vessel under Mexican registry for over 2 years. Pett also stated that the Troop family was from Glasgow as was the Irvine Family! This is inconsistent with my findings.

The *Annapolis Spectator* of July 22, 1898 carried the report that: "Frank Irvine, son of Alexander Irvine, Granville Ferry, is second officer of the transport ship *OSYABLE*, and was an eye witness to the destruction of Cervera's fleet. He says it was a sight never to be forgotten. His steamer is now in the blockade of Morro Castle. "

The above action took place during The Spanish American War of 1898, during which Admiral Pascual Cervera y Topete commanded the Spanish squadron sent to protect the colonies in the New World from the United States. He entered Santiago Bay, Cuba, May 19, 1898 where he was immediately blockaded by American Admiral Sampson's fleet. On July 3, Cervera followed orders and tried an heroic but unsuccessful escape from the enemy's blockade. Consequently, he lost all his ships and became a prisoner of war.

Morro Castle is a medieval castle that stood guard at the mouth of Santiago Bay in Cuba described as follows in 1898:

> At daylight one bright morning, July 1, the fleet steamed in front of the batteries and again silenced the enemies' guns and then for one time we started in to destroy Morro Castle. Although no guns were mounted there and it was a harmless piece of architecture, as the old stone mill at Newport, yet its appearance was tempting and an eyesore to the entire fleet and besides the colours of Castile floated from its flagstaff which seemed to aggravate the not over

meek temperament of the gunners and Blue Jackets. It was logically harmless, but sentiment sways the reason in war times and acting on the impulse, the OREGON sent a 13-inch shell towards the flag on that inoffensive flagstaff. When the smoke had cleared away, a great breach could be seen in the parapets of Morro and the flag and staff could be seen nowhere. Many a man in the fleet wished he could get his fingers on that striped piece of bunting; to secure it was out of the question. However, the colors were down and Morro was a smoking ruin and so nothing remained for the fleet but to steam out to their old stations and resume the blockade on Saturday the 2nd.

By 1935 Captain Frank Irvine's business address was 80 Wall Street in New York City and he was listed as among other things a specialist in Florida, Cuba, Mexico, Central and South America in "All Kinds Of Floating And Marine Equipment"; "Sole Eastern and Foreign Agent for Sandusky Boat Works" and representative for "Evinrude Outboard Motors" in Cuba and Mexico.

Frank's letterhead in 1935

In a letter dated February 15th, 1944 from Pastor Robert H. Dolliver of John Street Methodist Church in New York City to the President of Mexico, there is an account of Captain Frank W. Irvine being the guest speaker at the noonday service on the subject "Mexico and Her People". Also contained in this letter is the statement that "both of Frank's grandfathers attended this church nearly 100 years ago"! Frank's two grandfathers would be John Irvine and his mother's (Mary Piggott's) father, who is unknown. There is no indication of why John was in New York at that time, but it may have been to deliver a ship built by the Irvine Brothers.

Eva Estelle Irvine (1876-1957) *(John, John, Alexander)*

Violet Ethel Irvine (1880-1945) *(John, John, Alexander)*

John Alfred Irvine (1868-1928) *(John, John, Hugh Marshall)*

John Alfred Irvine

After growing up in Granville Ferry and going into the banking business, John Alfred (1868-1928) was a bank manager in Annapolis Royal before moving to Halifax, where he was employed as a clerk and then as accountant by Nova Scotia Building Society from 1887 to 1906. In 1906 he moved to Calgary, where he established a successful real estate and insurance business. He was an avid amateur photographer (Six albums of his photographs are preserved in the Nova Scotia Archives - some of the albums depict scenes of Halifax and vicinity and other Nova Scotia locations including Bear River, Clementsport, Granville Ferry and Smith's Cove.), one of the founders of the Canadian Navy League and active in the YMCA. He established a camp at Sylvan Lake, Alberta, on property he owned, which was used by the Boys Naval Brigade and other boys' and girls' groups. John Alfred married Mina Buckley of Halifax in 1901 and they had five children - **Hugh Avery (1905), Inez Abigail (1907), William Douglas (1910), John Alexander (Jack) (1913) and Wilfred Harland (1918).**

William Andrew Irvine (1870-1940) *(John, John, Hugh Marshall)*

According to the *Annapolis Spectator* of January 8th, 1897, Hugh's son, William Andrew (1870-1940) was a general dealer in dry goods, crockeryware, hardware, boots, shoes, rubbers, paints and oils.

Alton David (1874-1956) *(John, John, Hugh Marshall)*

The following is a note I received from Delmar Harrison, Alton David's grand son-in-law, who I have become acquainted with through our mutual interest in family genealogy and who has visited us in Nova Scotia. Del lives with his wife Julie in Qualicum Beach, BC, where Sylvia and I have visited with them.

> I am still curious about the Troop-Irvine failure. [12] If you ever come across info let me know.
>
> The Irvines seem to have been well off in the last half of the 1800's. But after this failure they appear to have been up against the wall. Hugh's oldest son, John seems to be the only one who did well financially. His real estate and insurance business in Calgary flourished and he was part of the Calgary establishment. He was president of the Navy League of Canada and ran for Parliament as a Liberal in the 1917 election. His brother Will was an alcoholic, who finally died in the provincial mental hospital in BC. My grandpa did well until the 1920's, but

---

[12] See Appendix 10 for the Annapolis Spectator article about closing the estate of Troop and Irvine

his business in Stavely depended on how the farmer's crops fared. He was generous with credit, but a couple of crop failures about 1926-27 bankrupted him. The family had to go and live with relatives in Calgary, I think brother John. Alton had a couple of mediocre jobs in Medicine Hat, until the early 40's, when he retired and went to live with his daughter, Doris, in Beaverlodge. In 1955, they came to live with us in Vancouver and he died the next year. They depended financially on their daughters, throughout their retirement. Anyway, no money ever passed down to us from the Irvines.

Mary Edna Irvine (1875-1963) *(John, John, John Edward)*

Mary Edna (Irvine) Angevine

Great Aunt Edna (1875-1963) married James Edwin Clarke Angevine (1873-1936) and they had four sons: **John Blackburn (Jack) (1902), Daniel Murray (1903), Edwin Douglas (1905) and James Stuart (1909)**. Douglas, who remained in Saint John in the family wholesale grocery business (Angevine and MacLauchlan), was the only one I knew as I stayed with Doug and his wife, Gwen, sometimes on weekends when I was going out with a girl from Saint John, while I was at University of New Brunswick in Fredericton. Doug and Gwen, had three children - **David (1937)**, who was at Mount Allison University while I was at UNB, continued in the business after his father died and now lives in Rothsay, NB; **Gerald (1941)**, an economist, who Sylvia and I once visited in the foothills of the Rockies outside Calgary, and **Mary Louise (1945)**, who died two months after being born.

Great Aunt Edna, a truly Victorian lady in her early 80s, was living in her house at 84 Sydney Street in downtown Saint John when I was at UNB and I visited her for tea a number of times.

An interesting connection of the Angevine family to Nova Scotia arose as I was doing the research for this narrative. My great uncle James E. C Angevine's great uncles, **John (1756-1828)** and **Peter (1759-1820)** Angevine settled in Ramsback, later known as Wallace, Nova Scotia, revealing an early connection of the Angevine family to Nova Scotia. In 1785, some 500 acres of land were granted to John (a record of the deed is in the Archives of NS, which lists John as a "Memorialist, who served as a volunteer in Colonel James DeLancey's regiment for several years before he came to this province at the conclusion of the American War.". The two brothers married sisters, with John marrying Sarah Amelia Carter and Peter marrying Mary Carter from Wallace. A nearby village was named Westchester after Westchester, New York, where the brothers were born. From 1800 until 1940 there was a great concentration of family in this area. The numbers have diminished, but there were descendents living on some of the property in 1960. The Angevine Cemetery in Wallace is on land of the original settler John and not far away is Angevine Lake.

William Henry Irvine (1878-1957) *(John, John, John Edward)*

William Henry (Harry) Irvine

I know little about Great Uncle Henry (1878-1957) or his wife Ada Mary Bryant, who was born in Malvern, Worchestershire, England in 1873. Henry and Ada lived first in Calgary and then in Toronto, where Henry was at one time District Manager for the Mutual Life Assurance company. The only information we have on Ada is contained in a letter from her Grandaughter, Carola, to me in 1994, as follows: "My father (Bryant) never threw anything away. Some of the saddest letters are those from and about Daddy's father. From what I have read and heard and what my Mother told me, his Mother (Ada) treated him very badly and really messed all their lives up. She was really a pretty difficult old lady. I think she caused a lot of unhappiness in the family, and I think greatly affected my Father's view of life and people."

We know more about Ada's father, Captain Nicholas Bryant, who was a Cornish mining engineer, who came from England with his family to the Londonderry iron mines in Nova Scotia in the 1870s. In 1881 the family moved to Alberta, where Mr. Bryant was sent by Sir Alexander Galt to prospect coal deposits near Coalbanks, which in 1885 became Lethbridge.

Arthur Marshall Irvine (1881-1952) *(John, John, John Edward)*

Young Arthur Irvine

The next direct descendent in our Irvine line was my grandfather, Arthur Marshall Irvine, who is the first ancestor that I knew to any degree. He was born in Saint John, New Brunswick on July 12th, 1881 and received his early education in the Saint John public school system until at age 17, in 1898, he started work with Saint John Iron Works as office boy. In his obituary, his career is likened to that of Horatio Alger, because 7 years later, at the age of 24, he was assistant to the manager. On the occasion of his marriage to Lulah Louise Craibe on June 3rd, 1905 the Company presented the couple with a chest of 30 pieces of splendid sterling silver cutlery, which they left to my parents, who passed it on to me as the eldest son.

On March 15th, 1906 their first child and my father, **Arthur Marshall Irvine Jr.**, was born into their house at 155 King Street East in Saint John.

Upon his departure from Saint John Iron Works Limited in 1907, Arthur and the family moved to 537 Prince Albert Street in Westmount, a residential neighbourhood of Montreal, where from 1907 to 1909 he was Secretary-Treasurer of the

Buffalo Forge Company. In 1909, he and a group of young Maritime businessmen took over the old Parker Foundry. They put the plant in order, carried on the foundry business and then started a steel plant.

Encouraged by their success, they acquired the Laurie Engine Company, fabricators of steel castings for railways and bridge companies.

In 1910 the Irvines moved a few blocks to 44 Windsor Avenue, the first home for their second son, **Lawrence Craibe Irvine**, who was born in September 2nd,1911.

Sometime before 1913 the family moved to 507 Grosvenor Avenue, but by 1914 they were living at 561 Roslyn Avenue. In 1917, they moved to 130 Arlington Avenue, then to 509 Clarke Avenue in 1920, where they remained until 1938. It is interesting that they moved as often as they did when these houses are within a few blocks of each other in Westmount. We know that at least three of them we have pictures of (Roslyn, Grosvenor and Clarke) were semi-detached, which would lead us to believe that at least those three, and perhaps all the various moves, were into rented houses. This would certainly confirm Grandpa's philosophy to always use other peoples' money wherever possible. He was a keen business man.

509 Clarke Ave.

In 1914 Arthur joined the Hudson's Bay Company, first as Assistant to the General Agent and a short time later as General Agent for all departments east of Winnipeg.

During this time, he travelled extensively in the north and accumulated an interesting collection of photographs of the polar expeditions of the ocean-going supply ship, *NASKOPIE*, and life of the aboriginal people. These are contained in three albums that I donated to the Manitoba Provincial Archives, in which the Hudson's Bay Company Archives is housed. In return, the Archives provided me with a CD of all the photographs in the albums, plus letters to and from Grandpa as the expedition was being carried out.

Through research carried out by the Archives, they have determined that as part of his duties as general agent, Arthur was directly involved with H.B.C.'s Moving Picture Expedition in 1919. As such he coordinated shipments of film and other supplies to and from the expedition crew, as well as ensuring that they were on track with proper itineraries and accommodations. It is likely that one of the three albums was gifted to Grandpa as an expression of appreciation for his involvement in the administration of the Moving Picture Expedition. The photographs in this album document the route followed for the filming of *The Romance of the Far Fur Country*. The photographs are representative of scenes from the film, including images of H.B.C. posts and staff, Inuit communities and modes of transportation in the early 20th century fur trade.

According to an article in the May 1921 issue of *The Beaver*[13], published for many years by H.B.C., in the fall of 1914 the French Government appointed H.B.C. purchasing agent in North America for goods

---

[13] See Appendix 11

required by the French military establishment during the First War. A separate agency, under Grandpa's direction, was set up in Montreal to handle this work. Later this arrangement was extended so that H.B.C. was entrusted with the purchase and transport of grain, flour and other foodstuffs, which the French government provided for civilian needs.

During the five years, 1915 to 1919, the quantity of goods transported in H.B.C. ships exceeded 13,000,000 tons. This contract with the French government was terminated on March 31st, 1921 at which time the Montreal Agency was disbanded and Grandpa left the employ of H.B.C.

The Beaver article ended with this paragraph: "The closing of the H.B.C. Montreal Agency at the termination of the French government contracts marks an epoch in the Company's history, during which it was privileged to render great service in the world war and at the outset of reconstruction".

Grandpa also collected northern native artifacts fashioned from narwhal tusks and other materials, some of which I have. In 1920, he and perhaps all employees, received a medal from the HBC commemorating the 250th Anniversary of that Company, whose history was so important to the development of Canada.[14]

After having spent about 17 years with industries and enterprises associated with iron and steel, and another 6 years with so widely different an organization as the Hudson's Bay Company, it was a surprise to all who knew Arthur when his next move in 1921 was to become a member of a Management Board

AMI Sr. at leisure

for a group of pulp and paper mills in Quebec. These included Saguenay Pulp and Paper Company, Bay Sulphite Company and another paper mill at Chandler, Quebec. But in 1924 he was back in the steel business as General Manager of coal sales for the British Empire Steel Corporation.

During these years and up until the time he retired, in addition to being busy climbing the corporate ladder, Arthur was heavily involved in the life of his community. He was a Justice of the Peace for the District of Montreal; a member of the Montreal Board of Trade; a member of the Council of the Family Welfare Association; member of the Federated Charities; First Chairman of the Boys' Naval Brigade Committee; on the Executive of the Quebec Branch of the Navy League of Canada; a Life Governor of both the Montreal General and Western Hospitals; on the Executive of the Montreal Sailors' Institute and President of the Maritime Provinces Club of Montreal. From a business standpoint, he served on the Council of the Canadian Institute of Mining and Metallurgy and the Executive of the Shipping Federation of Canada.

Times appear to have been good during this period because about 1913 Grandpa purchased a summer house at Thompson's Point on Lake St. Louis, along what is known as

[14] See Appendix 12

the Lakeshore west of Montreal at Beaurepaire. There the family spent their summers until about 1922, when Marshall was 16 and Laurie was 11. Although "out in the country" at that time, this location was very handy to downtown Montreal and it is interesting to speculate as to why they did not stay there. Many years later, in the early 1960s, when we lived further west along the Lakeshore in Ste. Anne de Bellevue, I visited Thompson's Point and identified the house from the pictures taken in the '20s. It was a substantial house very close to the Lake and must have been a fine place for young boys to spend their summers.

For whatever the reason they wanted a change, so in 1922 the Irvines purchased a vacation property in the Laurentians on Lake Manitou north of Montreal called "The Anchorage", which they owned until about 1940. I spent many happy summers there with my family, so have vivid recollections of the cottage and the surrounding property.

The BETTY

Lake Manitou, which was located southwest of Ivry Sur la Lac and west of Ste. Agathe des Monts, was quite a drive from Cornwall, especially travelling partly on gravel roads in Dad's Ford convertible with the open rumble seat, in which Monie and I made the trip! The main building was perched on the edge of Lake Manitou, with the lower floor at lake level being a boathouse, in which they kept a motor launch named BETTY, plus a canoe. From photographs of Dad and a "Betty" Brooks in 1926, we can surmise that perhaps the boat was named after her!

The upper floor contained at least four bedrooms, a large living-room that opened onto a balcony over the water, dining-room, kitchen and bathrooms. My recollection of the kitchen is centred on the brightly coloured dishes, which were Majolica ware or something very similar that were displayed on open shelves. Most of the furniture was of rustic design, the sort we had here in many of the cottages at Harbour View in Nova Scotia. This was a magical place to me as a child, because it had well-trodden paths all over the heavily

The Anchorage

AMI Senior, Mona Lou and David – Anchorage 1936

forested property. In one direction, a short distance from the house, a path took us toward the water to a small point of land where there was a tiny beach beside a gazebo; then in another direction winding through the mysterious woods, where I used to hold very tightly to my Grandmother's hand while we walked. In another direction, behind the house and up a bit of a slope was the driveway leading to a two-car garage.

One year I contracted the measles while we were at Manitou, so spent the time bundled up with my sunglasses on, playing in the sand or in the gazebo out at the point. Directly beside the house was a high, rock, retaining wall upon which we used to sit and watch the antics of the many large, green, bull-frogs at the sandy edge of the Lake below. We never figured out what the attraction was, but they were always there.

Grandpa retired at age 58 in 1939 from Dominion Steel and Coal Corporation, at which time he was Vice-President and General Manager for Coal Sales. That same year he and Grandma vacated the house at 509 Clarke Avenue and moved to Stanstead in the Eastern Townships of Quebec, where they rented a house called "Patton Place" from the Colby sisters, who were doyens of the community and lived in a very grand stone house across the street. "Patton Place" was a modest looking, white frame house, on another magical lot.

At least it seemed very special to a five-year-old at my stage in development. The house contained interesting rooms and furnishings; with the dining room being oak panelled to a high plate rail and the den and living room both having fireplaces that always seemed to be lit when we visited in the winter. The large lawn and garden area behind the house was surrounded by a very high cedar hedge, encompassing flower and vegetable gardens, plus a tiny "summer house" in which we played. I remember particularly the multi-hued hollyhocks that grew in some profusion along the hedge. Grandma showed us how to use the hollyhock flowers to make tiny dolls, with large hoop skirts.

During the Stanstead years Grandpa's car was a big, black LaSalle, in which he took considerable pride and kept polished like his shoes. When we were visiting Stanstead,

Monie, David and Grandparents - Stanstead

Grandma, Monie and I would sit in the back with a blue velvet rug over our laps while Grandpa drove. We felt very special. The car had two "jump seats" also, that folded down from the backs of the front seats, for children to sit on when the back seat was full of adults. As soon as we returned Grandpa would go over the whole car with a dust cloth before putting the car in the garage.

Also in 1939 their son, Lawrence, known as Laurie, was married and moved with his bride, Helen Simpson (1915-1998) of Toronto, to "Rolling Hills Farm", just outside Stanstead, which Grandpa had purchased for them. Uncle Laurie operated the farm until 1943, when he joined the Royal Canadian Artillery. I do not know whether Grandpa purchased the Farm so that Laurie and his family would be close to his parents, or visa versa?

Throughout the period he lived in Stanstead, Grandpa returned to the city by train on a regular basis to attend board meetings, as an officer and director of various companies. These included: Vice-President, Woods Manufacturing Co. Ltd.; Member of the Executive of The Fraser Companies Ltd.; and a Director of The Restigouche Co. Ltd., Reynolds-Coventry Ltd. and R&M Bearings Ltd. In Stanstead, he maintained his interest in his community by being a member of the Executive of the Eastern Townships Settlement Society, a trustee of Stanstead College and a member of the local Rotary Club.

Arthur Marshall Irvine - senior years

It is clear from such tributes as the following written by Jessie Colby to Grandma, at the time of Grandpa's death, that both he and Grandma were held in high esteem during their time in Stanstead: "I cannot think of one of you without the other, so true and constant and strong, so loyal to us all who have so loved you and relied on you and to all that we cherish in life. I am writing from my very heart and yet unable to express the smallest part of my love and gratitude. I long to see again, dear friend, and to have you understand what you have always meant and will always mean to us and to Stanstead. Simply looking across at Patton Place brings such thoughts, looking at the College, walking down the aisle to my pew - my dear your marks do follow you."

As a staunch Conservative, Grandpa was instrumental in forming the Progressive Conservative Association of Quebec in 1943. At a meeting at the Ritz Carleton Hotel in Montreal in January of that year, attended by the national party leader, Hon. John Bracken, Grandpa was named to the Executive and Mr. Bracken was named Honorary President of the Association.

It is interesting that my Dad, as the son of such a diehard Conservative, would marry my Mum, the daughter of such an active and dedicated Liberal as was my Grandfather McMaster. There must have been interesting discussions at the Irvine and McMaster dinner tables leading up to that union!

In the fall of 1947 the Irvines tired of rural living and moved back to Montreal and spent the winter in the Mount Royal Hotel. In the spring, they moved to Apartment #31 in the Acadia Apartment building at 1227 Sherbrooke Street West, across the street from the Ritz Carleton Hotel. Grandpa made his last monthly rent payment of $50.00 to Miss Jessie M. Colby for Patton Place on January 30th, 1948, and began paying rent of $143.00 per month to Montreal Trust, owners of the Acadia, on that same date.

Being the social person he was, with a multitude of friends throughout his life, Grandpa was, at one time or another, an active member of the Canada, Mount Stephen and St. James Clubs, the Royal Montreal Golf Club, the Royal Montreal Curling Club, the Royal St. Lawrence Yacht Club, and Rotary International. While he was travelling in the east he was a member of the Saint John Union Club and the Halifax Club. Each day in the later years, when I was aware of his habits, he would walk down Drummond Street to either the St. James Club or The Mount Stephen Club for lunch with his many friends.

Acadia Apartments

One day when I was about 14, I was visiting my grandparents at the Acadia Apartment, having travelled from Cornwall to Montreal on the train by myself under the watchful eye of the conductor. My friend, Colin Barclay, who had moved to Montreal after growing up a few houses from us on York Street in Cornwall, and I decided to go downtown to Eaton's, Simpson's and Ogilvy's on St. Catherine Street to check out the toys and particularly to ride the escalators. Coming from Cornwall, where the only store on more than one floor was MacIntyre and Campbell's Dry Goods Store, which had a mezzanine and an amazing vacuum system for handling invoices and payments between the clerks and the accounting office upstairs, I was impressed with those moving stairs and the elevators. At one point Colin and I decided to try to go UP the DOWN escalator, but were thwarted part way up by one of the clerks, who kicked us out of the store! But I digress, as the point of this story was to tell about Grandpa's toe rubbers, which I had borrowed since it was raining and my footwear was wet. We were supposed to be back at the apartment in plenty of time so that Grandpa could get to his lunch and I believe we were. The only problem was that the toe rubbers were soaking wet inside because they were a little large for my shoes and besides we had tested the depth of a few puddles on the way home! I perhaps have not mentioned that Grandpa was a natty dresser, who was very particular about his overall attire, which included shiny shoes attended to by various shoe-shine persons at his clubs or on the lower floor of the Mount Royal Hotel. As such it is not surprising that he was annoyed at me for defiling his rubbers and thereby disturbing his lunch routine. I think it was the only time that I experienced Grandpa being anything but good-natured, but Grandma Lou quickly used newspaper to soak up the water and after a short stay on the top of a high, cast iron radiator, the rubbers were satisfactory for Grandpa's use.

Not wanting to be in Montreal during the summer, and particularly in a stuffy apartment prior to air-conditioning, the Irvines rented a cottage at Moulinette, just west of Cornwall on the St. Lawrence River. One large and one small cottage on the same property overlooking the river, were owned by the Snetsinger family, who lived in Cornwall and operated a hardware store for many years on Pitt Street. Some years they were in the large cottage and some years in the smaller one depending on the use made of either by the Snetsingers. I was working at Howard Smith Paper Mill in Cornwall during some of those summers and used to ride my bicycle up to Moulinette to visit them.

During 1951 and the early part of 1952 Grandpa had been in and out of hospital for operations on his cancer, but was feeling well enough to go to Moulinette as usual to recuperate. They were in residence in the larger cottage in August of 1952 when Grandpa became very ill and was hospitalized, which explains why he died in the Cornwall General Hospital and not in Montreal on August 14, 1952. His funeral was at Erskine and American United Church, his home Church on Sherbrooke Street that he and Grandma had

Irvine Family Gravestone - Montreal

attended regularly for many years. He was buried near the top of one of many hillsides in Montreal's Mount Royal Cemetery.

The following tributes from two of his friends tell us what kind of a man he was:-

"I was saddened with the knowledge that my old friend had passed away. He had a magnetic, warm personality and radiated good cheer. I shall miss him very much."

"I cannot grasp the thought that dear Arthur is not here. He was always so active and cheery and possessed so many fine qualities seldom found in one person."

Lulah Louise (Craibe) Irvine (1881- 1957)

Lulah Louise (Craibe) Irvine

The saying, "Behind every successful man is a good wife", is a natural segue into the life of Lulah Louise Craibe, who married Arthur Marshall Irvine on June 3rd, 1905 in Centenary Methodist Church, later Centenary-Queen's Square United Church, in Saint John, New Brunswick. They were attended by Arthur's only brother, Harry, and Louise's best friend, Helen Frink, with the ushers being Dr. Harry Patton and John Hastie. Rev. George M. Campbell performed the ceremony. At the time, the bride and groom were both 24 years old, with Grandpa being 4 months the elder. Their first, and only home together in Saint John, was at 155 King Street East.

Lou, as she was called by family and friends, was born in Saint John, but unfortunately, we have no knowledge of her early life before she married Arthur.

Her Father, Francis Edward Craibe (1854-1915), known to all as Frank, was born in Saint John. Frank was a retail merchant who, at the time of his daughter's marriage, was working for the A. Chipman Smith and Company Ltd., a drugstore in Saint John. He later entered a partnership with William S. Barker, the son of H.W. Barker, whose store they took over at 35 King Street and renamed F.E. Craibe and Co., Druggists and Apothecaries. Lou's Mother was Alma Susan Roop (1855-1947), who was born and grew up in Saint John.

Lou had one older brother, Charles Walker Craibe (1878-1934), and as children they lived at 11 Orange Street in Saint John. In 1903, they moved to 80 Sydney Street, where Lou would have lived until she was married. Several early pictures we have, refer to her as Lulah. One at a very early age shows her on a swing beside her brother, Walker, while a later one is a photograph of a very sophisticated 10 or 11-year-old.

Except for some pictures, there is little information available on Grandma Lou in any family records. As such I can only draw on my limited recollections and those of others.

80 Sydney Street

I remember her as always well turned out in a dress, with her hair done, although I do remember in the later years, when they rented a cottage in the summer at Moulinette, she did wear tailored slacks sometimes. When I was young I thought of her as being very tall and I guess she was taller than most women. She also stood very straight and carried herself rather "queenly". Pinch-nez glasses were always perched high on the bridge of her nose.

Snacks at Grandma's house were graham crackers and a mixture of grape juice and ginger ale with ice cubes. She usually also let us have our favourite "twizzlers ", not the liquorice kind, but sticks of hard baked dough with worcestershire sauce drops on the outside. There were also always hard candies in a tall, round tin can.

The highlight of every trip to visit Grandma and Grandpa Irvine, when they lived in the Acadia Apartments on Sherbrooke Street, was a trip to the Themis Club, located further west on Sherbrooke above some commercial enterprise. It was a ladies' club that Grandma belonged to and she would take Monie and me there for lunch. I don't remember the first part of the lunch, but I do remember the dessert cart that was quite large and contained every kind of French pastry imaginable. That was my introduction to cream puffs, chocolate éclairs and especially napoleons! I was in heaven.

Following from the McCord Museum: "Organized in 1914 and incorporated in 1919, the Themis Club (1919-1981) was established as the first women's social club in Canada. In 1919, the club acquired a permanent establishment on Sherbrooke Street West. By the 1920s the membership reached 250 and the club established links with other women's clubs in Great Britain and the United States. Although the membership eventually grew to 650, a decline set in by the 1970s. The club's charter was abandoned in 1981".

Lulah Louise (Craibe) Irvine

Grandma did all her grocery shopping at Dionne's on St. Catherine Street, where we would walk from the apartment to select what was needed. Then we would walk home empty handed and the groceries would be delivered to the door shortly after we got home. Very civilized!

Although Grandma did some of the cooking when we were visiting, I think there was quite often a maid and a cleaning lady, who might have been the same person. I can remember there being a tiny bell to the right of Grandma's place at the dinner table, that she would ring to summon the maid. This was the case at both Stanstead and Montreal.

In Stanstead, the gardens were quite extensive and I recall that Grandma did at least some of the gardening, assisted by a man who helped around the property and house in many ways. The wood boxes for the four fireplaces were always full, the grass always cut and the driveway and walkways always clear of snow, and I know Grandpa did not do any of those chores.

Uncle Laurie's daughter, Wendy (Irvine) Plumb, recalls our Grammie Irvine as follows:

Grammie, I knew a little more because of the weekends I spent at their apartment after Grampie died. She seemed rather childlike. I recall that in watching TV, she thought that the people on the screen could see her just as we could see them. TV was very new then. I was 12 when Grampie died and we got our first TV for the coronation that year. She used to make a nice meatloaf. I loved the grape juice and ginger ale, also the cream and ginger ale. We used to walk down to Dionne's grocery store and also along St. Catherine to have "rainbow water ice" in a restaurant similar to Honey Dew. I don't remember the name of it. I think we played "go fish".

I don't know what her education was, but she didn't come across as educated. I never saw her read. She would set the breakfast table before going to bed each night. I don't remember what we ate for breakfast, but I do remember the toaster. It was one of those that the sides fold down and you turn the bread over to toast the other side. I still see them in antique shops.

I slept in Grampie's bed. When I think of it now, it makes me feel uncomfortable. I didn't like the guest room because of the fire escape right outside the window. She had extremely fine and thinning hair. She would roll the back hair around round rollers similar to what we use now. She used a lot of the old bobby pins. She would buff her nails and had a multi-piece silver nail care set on her dressing table."

Lulah Louise Craibe Irvine passed away in the Montreal Royal Victoria Hospital on 27 October 1957 at the age of 76, after suffering from mild dementia for a few years.

Roop Family Connection

I would like to digress from the Irvine family history for a moment to explore my connection to the Roop family who settled very close to our present family home in Smith's Cove and whose descendants remain in the area to this day.

Alma Susan (Roop) Craibe

My greatgrandmother, Alma Susan (my Nana Craibe and "Allie" to Roop relatives) was a daughter of John, granddaughter of Isaac Sr. and great granddaughter of Christopher Sr., who was originally from what is now Germany, but settled in Monmouth, New Jersey, after first arriving in NY about 1756. His first wife died on the passage. One Sally Greer traveling on the same ship stepped up to the plate and helped him with his four female children on the voyage. She was so good to them that he determined to marry her upon arrival. She then became Christopher Roop's 2nd wife and produced his 4 sons, Isaac Sr., John, Christopher Jr. and Jacob, who came to Nova Scotia with the spring Loyalist fleet on May 29,1784. Only Isaac Sr. and John remained, so all the NS & NB Roops of the Christopher Sr. line stem from them.

Alma Susan's mother and father and my 2x great grandparents, John H. Roop and Elizabeth Jane Wright, both of the Parish of St. John, were married by license on 16 December 1834, in Centenary Church, Saint John.

Following is Allie's mother's obituary from the *Saint John Globe* of Monday, April 4, 1904:

Mrs. John H. Roop died at the residence of her son-in-law, Frank E. Craibe on Saturday night age 80 years. She was a daughter of the late Wm Wright of this city, and was of Loyalist descent on both sides of the house. In 1832, she married John H. Roop of Digby who died in January 1883. She had 10 children of whom 3 daughters and 3 sons survive - Mrs. DeForest of New Jersy; Mrs. Dow Roop of Birkenhead, England, and Mrs. F. E. Craibe; J.W. and Henry H. Roop of this city, and Charles E. Roop, Truro, N.S. Mrs. Roop was held in high esteem.

Allie's uncle, James H. Roop, owned a large farm property at Roop's Point just east of Digby on the Annapolis Basin. Roop's Point formed the western shore of Joggins Brook, where it empties into the Annapolis Basin. Highway and railroad bridges have joined that Point to the eastern shore and the area is now known as Joggin Bridge, which is about three miles from where we live in Smith's Cove. Nana Craibe, as we knew her, visited her Uncle and Aunt as a young girl and described the property as follows in a letter dated April 15, 1942 to my Dad, who was overseas during the war: "It was an immense tract of land, given by Crown Grant of 100 acres, and more bought by my Uncle and Aunt Roop, who lived in the home some little distance from the road. Quite a large home, with outbuildings up from the home a distance, barns for horses, cows and I think hens. An immense orchard of apple, pear, cherry and plum trees and the grounds well grassed and kept in a lovely prosperous way. Of course, I was but 16 years old (1871) when I visited there. Had a lovely time - lots of cherries and cherry trees."

Recently I have discovered an overgrown family cemetery on the back end of the old Roop property, described above, containing some Roop graves and have taken steps to have it preserved and protected.[15]

Kenneth Inglis Irvine (1883-1883) *(John, John, John Edward)*

Helen Stuart (Nell) Irvine (1886-1980) *(John, John, John Edward)*

Helen Stuart (Irvine) Schofield

The second girl in the family was Helen, better known as Nell (1886-1980), who married Kenneth Rupert Schofield on October 16th, 1912. They had one daughter, Barbara, who was born Sept 11th, 1913.

At some point the Schofields moved to Montreal, where Barbara was born. Ken died there in 1962.

Aunt Nell died in Ottawa in 1980. The last time I can recall seeing Aunt Nell and Uncle Ken was at my sister Monie's wedding in 1960 in Cornwall.

I remember Ken as being a very dapper dresser. Uncle Ken was President and Chairman of Reynold-Coventry Ltd., a Canadian subsidiary of the British firm Ransome and Marles Bearing Co. Ltd. Both he and Grandpa Irvine served as board members of both companies.

---

[15] See Appendix 13 James H. Roop and wife graves - Roop family cemetary

FIFTH GENERATION

Hugh Avery Irvine (1905-1981) *(John, John, Hugh Marshall, John Alfred)*

Inez Abigail Irvine (1907-1998) *(John, John, Hugh Marshall, John Alfred)*

William Doughlas Irvine (1909-1972) *(John, John, Hugh Marshall, John Alfred)*

Enid Eileen Irvine (1912-1915) *(John, John, Hugh Marshall, John Alfred)*

John (Jack) Alexander Irvine (1913-2012) *(John, John, Hugh Marshall, John Alfred)*

Wilfred Harland Irvine (1918-1986) *(John, John, Hugh Marshall, John Alfred)*

Wilfred Harland (1918- 86) was born in Calgary. His main claim to fame from my point of view being his interest in genealogy. Granted this was prompted by his adherence to the Mormon faith, which requires all believers to search for and record all their ancestors. Many years ago, Harland corresponded with my Dad (Marshall) and later corresponded with me to fulfill his required quest. Through a roundabout process after Harland's death I contacted one of Harland's sons, **David Irvine (1956)**, who lives in Cochrane, a suburb of Calgary. David is a motivational speaker, who travels North America speaking to all manner of groups of people and has written numerous self-help books. We met once and continue to keep in contact from time to time via email. On one trip to Calgary, I borrowed Harland's "Book of Remembrance" from David, which contains the results of Harland's many years of genealogical research. It encompasses thousands of names, far and away beyond the limits of this story. Harland was married to Joyce Elinor Stewart (1921-1999) and they had another son, **Harland S. (1952-2017)**, a family doctor in Sundre, Alberta and a step-daughter, Kate.

Elizabeth Irvine (? -?) *(John, John, Hugh Marshall, William Andrew)*

William Irvine (? -?) *(John, John, Hugh Marshall, William Andrew)*

John R. Irvine (? -?) *(John, John, Hugh Marshall, William Andrew)*

Walter William Irvine (1905-b/f 1911) *(John, John, John Edward, William Henry)*

Kenneth Bryant Irvine (1907-b/f 1911) *(John, John, John Edward, William Henry)*

Henry Erskine Bryant Irvine (1909-1992) *(John, John, John Edward, William Henry)*

Bryant and Val with first cousin Jack Angevine

Henry and Ada had four children – **Walter William (1913, stillborn), Judith Elvira Ada Bryant Irvine (1912-32) Kenneth Bryant Irvine (1907-1910), Henry Erskine Bryant Irvine (1909-92)**. We know little about any of the other children, but a great deal about Bryant, who, after graduating from Upper Canada College, went to England to study law at Oxford. He was called to the bar in 1932 and served in the Royal Navy in WW II as a Lieut. Commander afloat and on land. On 4 February,1945 in Upton, Worcestershire, he married Valborg Cecilie (Carslund) Godman, originally from Fyn, Denmark, who had first married Thomas Ellison Godman, born 9 November 1915 in Steyning, Sussex, England, a naval officer, who was killed during WWII at Malta aboard *HMS HAVOCK*. Godman's family owned a large farm (318 acres) in Sussex, which surrounds a grand manor house named Great Ote Hall, that was built in the 15th century on the site of a previous dwelling called "de Otehall", built in the reign of Edward III in 1341.

Presumably there were no other heirs, so Val and Bryant took over the estate from the Godman family after their marriage and in the process, they changed their surname to Godman-Irvine. Val continued to actively manage the large property as well as another 609 acres nearby at Court Lodge until her death in February 1980, at which time their youngest daughter, Carola, took over. Val and Bryant adopted two daughters, **Jaqueline (Jaci)**, born 26 June 1948, who lives in Folkstone and **Carola,** born 6 November,1951, who lives at Ote Hall and manages the farm operation. Sylvia and I visited Carola at Great Ote Hall, and spent a night in one of the huge antique four-poster beds in a dark, wood panelled bedroom with leaded glass windows and a huge fireplace. The house is of special historic interest as it contains a pulpit built on by Selina, Countess of Huntington. The house is surrounded by formal gardens and farmland.

While I was growing up we used to receive Christmas cards from Bryant and Val, that normally had a picture of either Great Ote Hall or the parliament building on the front. As a child, I was quite impressed by both.

Carola and Jaci have been estranged for many years so I had been unable to be in contact with Jaci until a short time ago, when I located her through Facebook and learned she has recently re-married and is living

Great Ote Hall - Burgess Hill, Sussex

with her husband, Nicholas Hopes in Folkstone, on the Dover Coast of England. Nicholas is a professional scuba diver, who has a diving school. Jaci and Nicholas have plans to move to Panama, after they sell their house in Folkstone.

Henry Erskine Bryant Godman-Irvine

Always active in the Conservative Party, Bryant was Chairman of the Young Conservative Union in 1946-47, then rose to prominence as Chairman of the National Farmer' Union in 1954 and was elected to the British House of Commons as Member from Rye in 1955. While in the House for thirty-odd years he was active on many important committees as well as holding a number of offices in the Commonwealth Parliamentary Association from 1970-76, while he was Deputy Speaker of the House.

In 1982 Sir Bryant was named a life peer by the Queen in her birthday honours list and appointed to the Privy Council, an honour that normally went to cabinet ministers or judges of the Court of Appeal.

In 1959, while I was experiencing my eight months of travel, after graduation from UNB, Bryant arranged for my classmate and travelling companion, Ilbert Newcomb, and me to visit the House of Commons and have lunch with him in the Parliamentary Restaurant. The Prime Minister at the time was Harold MacMillan and we saw Sir Winston Churchill on the front bench in the House that day, although he did not speak. Our second meeting was in Halifax many years later, where quite by chance I saw Bryant being interviewed on television. I immediately called the

TV station and spoke to Bryant after he completed the interview. It turned out we were both staying at the Lord Nelson Hotel and had breakfast together the next morning. He was accompanied by his wife, Val, and daughter, Carola, but only Carola and Bryant joined Sylvia and Geoffrey and me for breakfast. After that Bryant and I maintained sporadic correspondence, as did cousin Wendy Plumb, by which I think he was happy to maintain some sort of contact with members of his Irvine connection.

Doris Margaret Irvine (1910-1930) *(John, John, Hugh Marshall, Alton David)*

Florence Elizabeth Irvine (1914 -2006) *(John, John, Hugh Marshall, Alton David)*

Lawrence Craibe Irvine: (1911- 1978) (*John, John, John Edward, Arthur Marshall*)

Laurie was born September 2, 1911 in Montreal. At that time, the family lived at 44 Windsor Avenue in Westmount. Photos indicate a chubby baby who looked more like his Dad than Mum.

Although the early pictures depict Marshall and Laurie together while they were young, it does not appear that they spent much time together after marriage and the cottage at Lake Manitou was sold in 1940.

Records are sketchy, but it is likely Laurie completed elementary school in Westmount and he attended Ashbury College in Ottawa for some period. Other high schooling is unknown, but perhaps he attended Roslyn High.

Wendy Jane (Irvine) Plumb's comments written in December 2012 about her Dad, are as follows:

Lawrence Craibe Irvine

> My Dad married Helen Irene Simpson on June 3, 1939 in Eglinton United Church, Toronto. Mother was born and raised in Toronto. Immediately following their honeymoon in Niagara Falls, they took up residence at Rolling Hills Farm south of Stanstead, Quebec. Dad had taken courses in animal husbandry at MacDonald College. I don't know why he decided to farm. He had a herd of Jersey dairy cattle and sold their milk to Carnation Milk. His hired hand lived in a house just down the road. On his 400+acres he grew oats and there was a sugar bush with a shack where maple syrup was produced each spring. There were also a couple of horses, pigs, a dog named Buddy and a cat (Dead Eye Dick) that was blind in one eye.

> I was born 27 April 1940. From the beginning, Dad and I had a special bond. He was a meticulous, orderly person and anything he did, he did well. In 1943 Dad joined the Royal Canadian Artillery and became an instructor at Petawawa, Ontario.

Laurie at Ashbury

He sold the farm and Mother and I moved to Toronto to live with her parents and sister in a four-plex on Avenue Road. My sister **Linda Carole Irvine** was born November 16, 1944. It became crowded in the four-plex and my grandfather bought a house in Lawrence Park that same year.

While at Petewawa Dad was involved in an overturned jeep accident in 1946 which left him with his back broken in two places. His life was never the same after that. Originally sent to Christie Street Hospital in Toronto, he was one of the first patients transferred to the newly-opened Sunnybrook Hospital in 1948. He spent time on a Stryker frame and wore a back brace for years. It consisted of vertical metals strips covered in leather. Quite a change from his former days of cross-country skiing and horseback riding.

In 1947, while he was still in Sunnybrook Hospital part time, Laurie began working in Toronto for Beamish Bag Division of Alliance Paper Co., where Grandpa had arranged a job through his friends Harold and Roy Crabtree. Dad bought a house at 244 Broadway Avenue (since torn down). **Robert Lawrence (Bob) Irvine** was born May 10, 1947.

In March of 1949 we moved to St. Lambert, Quebec (directly across from Montreal on the south shore), where Dad was Plant Manager, Woods Manufacturing Co., makers of jute and paper bags.

During his years in St. Lambert he also held positions as Manager of the Country Club of Montreal, Director of Civil Defense and Manager of the Roads Department. He belonged to the Lions Club and a men's club (probably called the St. Lambert Men's Club). One night he brought home for me some fried worms and chocolate-covered grasshoppers! I didn't touch them.

He was an excellent host at the Country Club and everyone liked him. I used to work in the office and when there was a tournament, he and I would sometimes go out for Chinese food after the cleanup. That would be about 2 a.m.!

Laurie about 1974

I cherished those times we spent together. He told me he dreamed of owning a fine dining establishment in the countryside. I would be the receptionist. His dream was never realized.

Sometime around 1960 my parents moved to a townhouse on Elm Avenue in Montreal, a block from Greene Avenue. After a few years, it was back to St. Lambert to live in an apartment on Riverside Drive. This was the last home they shared as Dad passed away February 10, 1978 at the age of 66. He died of his third heart attack and was alone at the time. Mother was in Toronto visiting her familly. An observant fellow tenant had noticed that Dad's morning newspaper was still outside his door in the evening and had notified the superintendent. The police had to knock down the door and found him dead in bed with his arms folded.

His ashes are buried in the Irvine family plot in Mt. Royal Cemetery, Montreal.

In 1968 my little family and I moved to Toronto and rarely saw my Dad after that. He never phoned or wrote. Strangely, two days after his funeral, my then 10-year-old daughter told me that he had called me the night before he died and I was out shopping. That phone call will haunt me the rest of my life.

My connection with my Uncle Laurie was almost non-existent because he and my father very seldom got together alone or as a family. Despite this, when Uncle Laurie died he left me his reproduction 1740 Charlesville flintlock musket, that had been presented to him upon his retirement as armourer at the Fort on St. Helen's Island from 1964 till 1974, along with a very attractive wooden toolbox that would have been his at the Fort. The musket has embedded in the stock the crests of the 78th Fraser Highlanders and Les Compagnies Franches de la Marine.

The present Fort was rebuilt during the War of 1812 and was the home of a French Company of Marines raised by Cardinal Richelieu in 1622, who served from armed merchant ships or as fort garrisons, and so became Les Compagnies Franches de la Marine. The Fort is also the Canadian home of the Fraser Highlanders, whose forebearers came from Scotland in the mid-1700s to fight for the King in Canada. Two regiments were raised, allowed to wear their strawberry kilts and fought with the English regiments at Louisburg, Quebec and Montreal.

And what of Laurie and Helen's three children? Wendy married Arthur George Plumb, who was born 9 January 1919 and died 28 February 2006, all in Toronto. They had one daughter, Jane Elizabeth Plumb on 14 February 1968, who married Lindsay Neil Pearlman (1ST) on 20 June 1991 and since divorced. They had Hannah Meryl Pearlman 22 June 1994 and Jonah Michael Pearlman on 30 September 1997. Jane married (2nd) Rodney Yale Kaufman (1967). Wendy lives in an apartment in Toronto, a few blocks away from Jane and her family.

Carole married (1st) Clifford Kurz, which lasted only a few years, followed by her marriage to fellow musician, Manfred Eberhardt Liebert, born 31 December 1934 in Woelfersheim, Germany. They have lived in Germany for many years, but occasionally return to Canada and visited us in Nova Scotia some years ago. Carole taught music for a number of years, while both she and Manfred have played and perhaps are still playing in several symphony orchestras in Germany.

Tragically, Robert Lawrence (Bobby) took his own life 6 September 2001 at the age of 54.

Arthur Marshall Irvine (1906 -1970) (*John, John, John Edward, Arthur Marshall*)

Baby Marshall

As described in a lovingly kept baby book, given to Marshall by his Nana Craibe at Easter 1906, Marshall was born at 6:45 pm, on 15 March 1906, in the first bedroom off the hall, lower floor, 55 King Street East in Saint John, New Brunswick. Dr. P. Robertson Inches was the attending physician and the baby weighed seven and one-half pounds. Marshall was baptized on 15 May 1906.

Grandparents and aunts were plentiful at the christening, with the result that many special presents were received by the babe. His Grandfather Craibe was particularly generous with both a gold ring, set with three little stones and a pair of white kid boots.

On the 17th of August 1907, when Dad was 18 months old, he moved with his parents to Montreal, where their first house was at 537 Prince Albert Avenue in Westmount. In September, he was in poor health, which is indicated as being caused by the change in climate and in November he had chicken pox for three weeks. He contracted whooping cough in January of that year which continued until June.

From the fall of 1908 until fall 1909 he enjoyed perfect health, but in October 1909 he fell over the railing of the steps at 44 Windsor Avenue and was unconscious for 24 hours! Interestingly, none of us ever heard about this from Dad and learned it just recently from his Baby Book.

Early summers appear to have been spent back in New Brunswick visiting Grandparents and other relatives in Hampton and Saint John.

Dad attended his first Church service with his parents at St. Andrew's in Westmount in April 1909, and then later that summer in July at Centenary Church in Saint John with his Nana Craibe. There is an indication that he attended Sunday School but, no dates are recorded.

Marsh at Rothesay

While he must have had playmates in Westmount, the list in the baby book covers only his summers from 1906 to 1910 back in New Brunswick. Early birthday parties were attended by mostly adult relatives, but by 1910 when he was four, the party held from 4 to 6:30 o'clock was attended by 20 little children!

Dad's baby brother, Lawrence Craibe Irvine, was born September 2nd, 1911 at 44 Windsor Avenue.

For some unexplained reason, Dad began his early education at Roslyn Avenue School on January 1st, rather than early September 1912. He was two and a half months short of his 6th birthday. It may have had something to do with the family moving from Windsor Avenue to 507 Grosvenor Avenue, where they lived until 1914, when they moved again to 561 Roslyn Avenue. Then on October 1st, 1913 he was attending Aberdeen School in Montreal West, until his 7th birthday when he travelled to Saint John with his father and contracted measles. He remained in Saint John with his Nana Craibe for two months and was tutored by a Miss Rainnie, who would have been a Craibe relative.

Also in 1913, Grandpa Irvine purchased a summer home on Thompson's Point, at Beaurepaire, on the Lakeshore west of Montreal, where the family spent the summers until 1920 when they purchased the Anchorage on Lake Manitou in the Laurentians.

By September of 1914 the family had moved to 561 Roslyn Avenue and he was back at Roslyn Avenue School, where he remained until 1919. In 1917 the Irvines moved to 130 Arlington Avenue, where they lived until 1920. Two Roslyn class pictures show him as being taller than most of his classmates, with his hair parted slightly off to the right of the centre of this head. Later pictures indicate he maintained this hair style at least until after his McGill days, probably altering it to a more "normal" style when he went to work in Shawinigan.

On September 12th, 1919, at the age of 13, Dad began his life away from home, when he was enrolled at Ashbury College in Ottawa. Unfortunately, we do not know if there was some reason for this change, other than that in those days sons of wealthier families went to private school.

From the beginning of his days at Ashbury, Dad was involved in all aspects of school life and appears to have flourished in the process. There is no record of him being active in sports at Roslyn School, but it can be assumed that he must have been, as he excelled immediately at Ashbury. In his first year as an Intermediate, he placed first in the 100-yard dash and 3rd in the 880-yard run and along with a friend won the doubles tennis.

In succeeding years, he competed in cricket, soccer, hockey, basketball, skiing, gymnastics and football, and was Captain of many of his teams. In track and field, the shorter events - 100, 220 and 440 yards were his specialties, however, he also placed well in the 880-yard, 120-yard hurdles, and high jump events. In 1923, he set a school record in the 440-yard run. Up to his graduation in 1924, he was the only one in the history of the school to win the Fleming Cup for all-round proficiency in Senior sports three years in a row.

Cricket Team Captain 1923

In addition to his accomplishments in sports, he was a bugler in the Cadet Band in his first year; won the Cox Cup for Junior Rifle Shooting in his second year and then went on to be the Commanding Officer of the Cadet Corps. and Head Boy in his last year. That year he was awarded the Nelson Shield for the "Keenest sense of duty "in the Corps. This is the same award that his granddaughter, Jennifer Roope Irvine, won in her last year at King's-Edgehill School in Windsor, Nova Scaotia, when she was second-in-command of her Cadet Corps. and Head Girl of the school. Her Grandfather would have been very proud of her.

Academically he was awarded the 3rd prize for General Proficiency in both his third and fourth years. A complete list of Dad's accomplishments while at Ashbury can be found on the back inside cover of his baby book. It appears to be in his handwriting.

Following is an excerpt from a letter his Principal, Rev. George P. Woolcombe, wrote to Marshall's parents at the time of his graduation from Ashbury in the Spring of 1924," I feel I must tell you how very pleased I have been with his general conduct and attitude during the whole of his course here. Never once has he been guilty of any serious infractions of the rules, he has always been absolutely reliable and loyal, and his influence since he has been Captain of the School has been of the very best. He has been a great help to me personally and I shall miss him very much indeed. I have never had a boy who was more generally satisfactory pass through this School. I wish him every possible success and happiness in his future career, and I know that he will turn out a just and useful man."

Sometime after he left Ashbury, Dad donated "The Irvine Cup", to be awarded annually to the winner of the Junior Boy's Cross-Country Race.

In 1920 the Irvine family moved from Arlington Avenue to 509 Clarke Avenue, where they remained until 1938.

Mona and Marsh 1930

During his summers while at Ashbury, Dad worked at a variety of jobs. Summer of 1922 he was a Testman in the laboratory of the Ha Ha Bay Sulphite Ltd. at Port Alfred, Quebec and in 1923 he worked in the Efficiency Department of La Compagnie de Pulpe de Chicoutimi at Chandler, Quebec.

In the fall of 1924, Dad enrolled in the Mechanical Engineering Faculty of McGill University in Montreal. He joined Kappa Alpha Fraternity and was active in intramural sports until he left the University in 1927. Continuing after Ashbury to be active in track and field events, Dad equaled the Canadian indoor 60-yard dash record in 1926 at an Inter-Faculty meet in the Craig Street Drill Hall in Montreal.

The reason for his leaving before graduation in 1928 is unknown, but it may have had something to do with his father's financial situation. There was always an indication that Grandpa Irvine was wiped out in the Crash of `28, although considering how well he did in later years, this story might not have any validity. Unfortunately, it is one of those mysteries that will never be solved.

Regardless of why it happened, Dad left McGill and began his full-time working career in June 1928 in the Engineering Department of Shawinigan Chemicals in Shawinigan Falls, Quebec, at a salary of $125.00 per month. On January 1st, 1929, this was increased to $135.00 per month.

For the previous three summers he had worked, first as a draughtsman in the Aeroplane Department of Canadian Vickers Limited, Montreal; next in re-enforced concrete construction with Fraser, Brace Engineering Company at Farmer's Rapids, Quebec; and finally, in boiler erection and testing with the Combustion Engineering Company at Ste. Anne Pulp and Paper Company, Beaupre, Quebec and Laurentide Mill, Grand`Mere, Quebec.

Somehow during his various terms of employment, and I'm sure with some help from his parents, Dad purchased a new 1930 Ford Roadster. It had a foldout rumble-seat, which is where Monie and I sat when we drove up to the Anchorage to visit our Grandparents when Monie was 4 and I was 2.

Marsh and 1930 Ford

On March 3rd, 1931 Dad married Margaret Mona McMaster, daughter of Hon. Andrew Ross McMaster and Florence Bellhouse (Walker) McMaster in Montreal and they moved to Shawinigan to begin life together in an apartment at 31 Connaught Avenue.

On June 23rd of that year Marshall lost his job due to cutbacks caused by the depression. He was being paid $160.00 a month and facing a 5% reduction on July 1st.

Times were tough for the newly married couple for the next few years while they lived in Notre Dame de Grace and Dad spent a year working for Nichols Engineering and Research as a Mechanical Draughtsman in Montreal and Three Rivers, Quebec, at a salary of $175.00 per month and part of a year with McColl-Frontenac Oil Refinery in East Montreal as a Lab Assistant and Labourer. He left in May 1933 to join Howard Smith Paper Mills Limited in Cornwall, Ontario as a Lab Assistant and Time Study Trainee at a salary of $125.00 per month, the same amount he was making as a single man just out of university, five years earlier! After a general staff increase of 5%, he was making $131.25. Times were still tough.

During this rather challenging period in the young couple's life together, their first child, **Mona Louise**, was born in Montreal on February 22nd, 1933.

Upon arrival in Cornwall in the spring of 1933, the Irvine family rented the centre unit of a brick, three bedroom, semi-detached house at 243 York Street, on the corner of York and Third Streets, where we were to remain for the next 16 years. The building was owned by Mr. and Mrs. Williams, who lived in a large brick house next door on Third Street. There is no record of the monthly rental cost at that time, but I do remember it was $40.00 by the time I was old enough, during the war, to deliver rent cheques across the back driveway and lawn to the William's house. The rental included the middle garage, in a row of three, at the back of the house.

243 York Street, Cornwall (centre unit)

By 1934, Dad had been promoted to Supervisor of Standards and Time Study and in 1935 he changed Departments and became a Cost and Accounting Clerk. In 1936, he spent two months being trained in the Montreal Order Office and on his return to Cornwall was appointed Cost and Order Supervisor during 1936-37. The following is from a letter to the Cornwall Mill Manager, Brydon Milledge, regarding arrangements for Dad's time in Montreal: "...it has been decided that in making transfers of staff of this nature, for the education of the person concerned, that the Company will pay one return fare from Cornwall to Montreal and a living allowance of $ 40.00 per month while in Montreal. If Mr. Irvine wishes to go back to Cornwall during this period he will have to pay his own fare."

Stepping back to 1935, a new addition to the family arrived at Cornwall General Hospital on November 11th in the person of me, **David Marshall Irvine**. The small front room, which Dad had used as an office, became Monie's bedroom, with me in the bedroom next door and Mum and Dad at the back next to the bathroom.

In the late fall of 1937 the Ford was valued at $150.00 when traded in on a 1935 Plymouth Coach costing $500.00. An additional $100.00 cash was paid at time of sale, with the balance to be paid by 10 monthly installments of $25.00.

By way of a correspondence course through the International Accountants Society, he obtained a Diploma in Office Management in 1937, which lead to his promotion to Office Manager for Cornwall Mill in 1938.

2nd Lieut. Marshall Irvine, 1942 London

With the threat of war with Germany looming, Dad joined the NPAM (Non-Permanent Active Militia), Stormont Dundas and Glengarry Highlanders Infantry Regiment in Cornwall in 1938 as a Platoon Commander with the rank of First Lieutenant. Sometimes referred to as "Weekend Warriors", Dad's association with the Militia continued until 1940 when he went into Active Service.

As Office Manager from 1938 to 40, Dad completed a Pulp and Paper Course via correspondence in 1939.

Although busy with a young family, working full time during the day and the militia some evenings and weekends, Dad still managed a full social life with friends, many of whom became life-long friends. Mum and Dad were active in Knox United Church, where they played tennis and badminton.

Not forgetting his two alma maters, Dad continued contact throughout his life with and supported financially the Kappa Alpha Alumni Association and The Ashbury College Old Boy's Association.

Travel was limited with small children, but we still drove in the roadster and later in the 1935 Plymouth to Dad's parent's cottage, the Anchorage, on Lake Manitou in the Laurentians, visited Mum's family in Montreal, Knowlton (in the Eastern Townships, south of Montreal) and Newaygo (in the Laurentians, north of Montreal) during those dying years of the "dirty thirties".

Dad also enjoyed sailing with his good friend, Neil McGillis, on Lake St. Charles east of Cornwall.

The Irvine family's affiliation with Knox United Church spanned the years before and after the war, continued until we all left Cornwall, and was resumed when Mum and Dad moved back. Over that period, Dad was an Elder and served as both a member and an officer on the Trustees and Board of Management. Mum was instrumental in forming the Friendship Circle for younger women, as an offshoot of the WMS (Women's Missionary Society) and in developing a Sunday Nursery School for toddlers, like youngest brother Doug was at that time. Monie was a teacher in the Nursery School.

On 26 August 1939 Dad went active with the rank of Second Lieutenant when the Regiment was called out to Canal Guard duty, one week before War was declared.

Just prior to being shipped overseas in the summer of 1940, the Regiment was posted to Debert Camp near Truro. Dad and several of his fellow officers rented cottages on the high banks above the shore of the Minas Basin near Bass River so our families could be near enough that the soldiers might be with us on weekends and other special leaves. The Grays (Bob, Margie and Michael) were next door to us and other friends, Janet, Reg and daughter Betty Baker were beyond them. There were long stairs down to the beach in front of the cottages, where we spent long hours swimming and walking out on the mud flats at low tide. Sometimes the Officers would bring some of their troops out to the area for a picnic and a swim and we would get to ride in the jeeps and the motorcycle sidecars. Neat stuff for a five-year-old.

On at least one occasion the Regiment paraded through the streets of Truro, complete with pipe band, and tiny Michael Gray with a Glengarry on his head, saluted the troops as they marched past us.

Dad's parents, Grandma and Grandpa Irvine, drove down to Nova Scotia and stayed for a time in a hotel in Truro and came out to Bass River each day to see us and their son when he was available on weekends.

Although I lived through the war years, I am not as accomplished a military historian as my son, Geoffrey. As such, the following impressive account of his Grandfather's active military career has been written by Geoff.

The military history of Lt. Colonel Arthur Marshall Irvine, MBE, CD

Arthur Marshall Irvine served his country with pride and distinction in World War Two. Marsh was 35 in July of 1941 when he sailed out of Halifax harbour as a platoon commander with his home regiment, the Stormont, Dundas and Glengarry Highlanders (S, D and G's), volunteers from those three eastern Ontario counties.

He was too old to expect to stay with the regiment when they would face combat on Juno Beach three years later in 1944 and he was too young to have been in the trenches of the Great War. Marsh was destined to play a unique and distinctive role in the ultimate allied victory that would impact his family and his personal life until he died very young in 1970.

It was partly due to his age and his previous civilian experience that Marsh experienced a much different war than the majority of his peers. During his five and a half years of active service Marsh was a platoon commander and regimental adjutant with the S, D and G's, Staff Captain logistics with HQ 1st Canadian Corps and HQ 2nd British

Marsh in Holland 1945

Visiting home - Stanstead, Quebec - Oct. 1940

Army, a student back home at Royal Military College for #7 Canadian War Staff Course, Deputy Assistant Quartermaster General with the Canadian section of BUCO (build up control organization) West in HQ 21st Army Group (British), General Staff Officer (GSO 2 Major) Liaison with HQ 1st Canadian Army and GSO 2 Liaison and Officer Commanding the Administrative Liaison section of 1st Canadian Army.

Through this five and half years he would train and serve in Cornwall, Kingston and Ottawa, Ontario; Debert and Windsor, Nova Scotia; throughout southern England; spend long periods of time in London and then move just behind the fighting through France, Belgium, Holland and Germany. He would father a son; spend part of the summer of 1941 (while training at Debert) in a cottage in Bass River, NS with his family; come home to Canada for the staff course at Royal Military College; write hundreds of letters home; worry about his three children, Mona Lou, David and John (conceived at the end of #7 CWSC and born on July 3, 1944) and wife Mona at home; visit the coast of England, London, Paris and Brussels on leave; feel guilty that he was not "with his boys" in the S, D and G's on the front lines; work harder than he ever had or would in his life and complain very little. He came home and continued to do his duty, becoming a Lt. Colonel and Commanding Officer of the now militia S, D and G's in the 1950's and going back to a normal, quiet postwar Canadian life.

The following tells the military story of Arthur Marshall Irvine Jr.

The Stormont, Dundas and Glengarry Highlanders – In Canada

Glengarian's Cap Badge

Sensing that war was possible and determined to play his part in the defense of freedom, thirty- two-year-old father of two, Marsh Irvine joined the Non-Permanent Active Militia (NPAM) regiment the Stormont, Dundas and Glengarry Highlanders on September 8, 1938. After a year of training on weekends and the situation deteriorating in Europe, the militia was activated with Marsh's first duty to guard the St. Lawrence river canal locks for two weeks at the end of the summer of 1939. More light training ensued for the next 10 months with full mobilization taking place on June 18th, 1941. The regiment was comprised of various units from Peterborough, Kingston and Cornwall, Ontario. Cornwall supplied the men for company's C and D and the band. Lt. Marsh Irvine was among the first officers to command C and D companies that included Lt. Allan McMartin, Capt. Eddie Hall and Marsh's lifelong friend, Capt. Bob Gray (Bob would also enjoy a non-traditional war

experience leaving the regiment to become a historical officer with First Canadian Army). The summer and fall of 1940 were spent securing uniforms, getting inoculated and all the minutia of building an army from scratch. Marsh enjoyed this work and this attention to detail and staff work would foreshadow his work later in the war. The regiment first spent time training at the Barriefield ranges in Kingston, a three-hour drive from Cornwall. On November 6th, the battalion left for Ottawa and took up quarters at Lansdowne Park (home of the present day CFL football team Ottawa Redblacks) where they began more advanced infantry training including using Bren gun carriers at the Connaught ranges. While in Ottawa the officers of the battalion were hosted for dinner by MP's from eastern Ontario ridings and their wives for two tea dances at Rideau Hall.

On January 29, 1941 Marsh began his return to his Maritime place of birth (he was born in 1906 in Saint John, NB) as the regiment headed for their final domestic training experience and boarded a train bound for Camp Debert, NS. The entire 9th Canadian brigade (North Nova Scotia Highlanders and Highland Light Infantry of Canada were the other two

On parade - Kingston, Ontario - Oct 1940

units in the only completely highland unit) was assembling at the sprawling rural base for final training before proceeding overseas. Marsh noted in his diary of January 27, "Had a nice day at home with my family. Rather sad at heart but tried not to let it show. Each one played the same game and we had a happy time. As the time for leaving draws nearer the tears become more acute. May they be spared the horrors of war even if they live to be a ripe old age". The train dropped the men off at Belmont Station followed by a twenty-minute march through and into the new barracks. I drive this route often to go skiing and think every time about Marsh and the men marching down the same streets so long ago.

The regiment trained all winter through the cold and wet Nova Scotia weather and Marsh spent time in Truro playing hockey, attending lectures and managing his platoon in company D. From the February 8 diary, "very cold, trained 200 men for war savings parade in Truro tomorrow. Changed orderly officer with A.A. McMartin. Had lecture on map reading from Capt. Christensen. Bought rubber boots $4.05". Even though the battalion had only been away from Ontario for a couple of months the transition for Marsh and his family was difficult, a similar circumstance for all of

Mona and Marsh - Nova Scotia 1941

the men getting used to the harsh reality of being a soldier. From March 3, "more snow but fairly mild and raw. This is about third wedding anniversary away from Mona. Ten years married today. Regimental meeting all evening".

In July, it was time for the 9th brigade to leave Canada for further advanced training and Marsh and his men were trucked to Halifax where they boarded *HMS ORION* for the voyage to England. They arrived at Avonmouth, UK, on July 30 after a nine-day voyage and took up quarters at Barossa Barracks at Camp Aldershot.

Fred Lander, Archie MacDonald and Marsh Irvine at sea, July 1941

The Stormont, Dundas and Glengarry Highlanders – In the United Kingdom

The regiment stayed at Camp Aldershot for less than three months and began their nearly three-year time of training and preparing for their role in the invasion of France in 1944. During the fall of 1941 the regiment began basic training with route marches; simple battalion schemes; individuals went off on courses in Cipher, Passive Air Defence, Concealment, Camouflage, Rifle training and in November, amphibious operations. To keep the men busy and their minds alert there was always a strong focus on sports including lacrosse, touch rugby, ping-pong (one of Marsh's favorites), darts, track and field, volleyball, soccer and softball.

Their Majesties inspecting 3ʳᵈ Canadian Division - September 1941

King George VI and Queen Elizabeth inspected the 3ʳᵈ Canadian Division in September. The S, D and G's were a member of the 9ᵗʰ Brigade – the Highland Brigade, three infantry divisions strong including the North Nova Scotia Highlanders and the Highland Light Infantry of Canada and had the honour of supplying the pipers who played for their Majesties. Queen Elizabeth asked one of the pipers what his brass shoulder badge *Glengarrians* was short for. The Corporal replied that it was short for "Stormont, Dundas and Glengarry", to which the Queen replied, "I am glad you use the word Glengarrians!". [16]

The first Christmas away from home was spent in billets in Middleton where the regiment had moved in early December. The holiday was difficult for all and would be the first of four for Marsh away from Mona and the children. As has always been the case throughout history, armies and men far away from home make the best of it with the officers serving the men dinner and then many being invited out to civilian homes for a more traditional family meal.

---

[16] See Appendix 14 For Cornwall newspaper article dated September 2, 1941

The regiment left Middleton in early January 1942 and moved to the Selsey Bill area, near Chichester which signalled the regiment's first operational role as a defense force protecting the UK from seaboard invasion by the Germans. Strong points equipped with machine guns and anti-tank weapons were manned on a 24-hour basis.

Christmas dinner 1941–Lt. Bob Gray in foreground, Marsh serving at back, right.

Marsh continued to command 18th Platoon and was kept busy as close liaison was established between the Canadians and the Sussex Home Guard to ensure that they had a strong sense of comradeship and understanding in case of a German invasion. It was in this liaison role that Marsh likely started to be noticed by his superiors as someone who could play a leadership role in the army that would re-take the European continent two years later.

The coming of Spring meant intensive training in large scale operations that included Exercise Beaver IV (a scheme that had 3rd Division in defence against 2nd Division acting as a German invading force) and Exercise Tiger. "Tiger" was a Corps Exercise with British troops involved that took place mostly at night and tested

Lt. Fred Cass, Lt. Rod McAlpine, Lt. Marsh Irvine – Spring 1942

the endurance of all. Marsh and his men marched over 185 miles, slept during the day and spent much of the week "fighting" in the pouring rain. In early June Marsh and "D" Company moved into Buxted Park to train with the 18th Sussex Battalion of the Home Guard.

Exercise "Harold" took place during the last part of July with 3rd Canadian Division acting as an invading force landing on the Continent with the 46th British Division playing the Germans.

Leaving the S, D and G's – Headquarters 1st Canadian Corps

1st Canadian Corps

**Pat Petepiece, Marsh, Charlie McGuire and Perc Milligan
August 31, 1942**

With the regiment's move to Denne Park Camp in early August, 1942, Marsh's war was about to change dramatically. With the Dieppe Raid about to take place, the Canadian Army was embarking on a period of growth in preparation for the eventual large-scale invasion of France. Older Officers who had been early volunteers and had been with their original regiments were being carefully evaluated for their abilities and skills that would form the senior officer corps that would take the Army to fight, whenever that time would come. Given Marsh's age, ability as a skillful and meticulous administrator before the war and with the Corps staff depleted due to the Dieppe raid, he was chosen to become a Staff Learner, promoted to Captain and transferred to 1st Cdn. Corps Headquarters. 1st Canadian Corps was the command structure that encompassed the 1, 2 and 3rd Canadian Infantry Divisions with attached machine gun, reconnaissance, anti-tank, mortar, anti-aircraft and affiliated units.

A.A. McMartin, Marsh Irvine and Capt. R.F. Gray

In his book "The Politics of Command", Lt. General A.G.L. McNaughton (who Marsh worked for and with during this time), noted that, "It has been the policy to appoint selected regimental officers as Staff Learners on the staffs of various formations and headquarters of the Canadian Army overseas in order not only to determine their aptitude for staff employment but also to give them practical experience in the field".

It was during this time that Marsh developed lifetime friendships with officers including Major Jack Clunie (who he would mention dozens of times in letters home), Captain George Harris, Ernie Whelpton, Sandy Somerville, Jim Grandy and many other who were brought together from their home regiments to make the core team of officers that would work together to make 1st Canadian Corps a potent fighting force.

Front Row: Jack Clunie, Graham Robertson, Marsh
Back Row: Doug MacDonald, Ernie Whelpton
Jim Grandy, Sandy Somerville

During the fall of 1942 and winter/spring of 1943, Marsh was actively involved with the management of logistics for Corps HQ during major training operations including Exercise "Curly Kate I", "Welsh II" and the largest operation to date, GHQ Exercise "Spartan".

Activities in late April and early May included intensive travel to visit 2nd Canadian Division units, artillery exercises and an engineer workshop for a week. It was during this time that Spring flowers were beginning to show and Marsh told Mona in a letter, "It was wonderful walking through the woods on the way home at lunch with all the different blossoms, I only wish I could smell them. My power of smell has completely left me and is has been months since I have been able to smell anything". On the way back Marsh stopped at Oxford and a cooked lunch in the cafeteria at the historical college, saw the movie "Strike up the Band" and enjoyed dinner at the Chesterfield Officers Club.

It was during this period that he was promoted to Staff Captain "Q" (Logistics) and chosen to be sent home to Canada to attend the next staff course, # 7 Canadian War Staff College from June until November. Letters during that time show the excitement that Marsh felt thinking about seeing his family after being away for almost two years. While awaiting his departure in London, Marsh spent a quiet week at a transit camp, eating, sleeping, reading and walking every day, a welcome change from the intensive working, travelling and training he had been doing for months. On the last night, he attended a dance with Capt. Rod MacAlpine, his wife and sister who Marsh told Mona was, "very plain, almost ugly but quite pleasant".

A chance to go home - # 7 Cdn. War Staff Course at Royal Military College (CWSC)

The men of Marsh's generation took their newfound roles as military officers very seriously and were keen for promotion and advancement. Many had been professionals in private life and as such approached their time in the military as an extension of their civilian careers. Everyone wanted promotion, an opportunity for increased leadership responsibility and recognition for their efforts. Of course, a great many stayed in the military after the war and enjoyed long and happy careers but for people like Marsh, an above average committed citizen of Canada, he felt that if he was going to make the sacrifice to be away from his family and do his duty, he had better do the very best job he could and advance through the ranks to the best of his ability.

For aspiring officers like Marsh one key step in that process was to be chosen to further his studies at an advanced military staff college. Some Canadians were chosen to attend a staff course in England at Camberley or if lucky, return home to attend one of the courses at Royal Military College in Kingston, ON. As luck would have it, Marsh had made a name for himself, was well known for his abilities and was expected to play a leading role in preparing the Canadian Army for the invasion of France and ultimate victory.

Marsh Irvine during demonstration - #7CWSC

The staff course prepared hundreds of Canadian officers for what lay ahead as the end of the war and the defeat of Germany was contemplated. Officers studied defence and offensive operations, artillery, invasion tactics, the principles and theory of war and dozens of other key topics necessary for senior officers to learn and understand.[17]

From all accounts, the summer and fall spent at RMC were enjoyable from a professional standpoint and Marsh could spend leave time with Mona and the children in Cornwall and in Kingston. At the end of the course Marsh received some much-needed leave and then once again boarded the train in Montreal for the trip to # 1 Transit Camp in Windsor, NS and eventual placement on a ship from Halifax. He spent a week in Windsor and his letters home that week are a mixture of practical information about what he did (movies, exercise, training, visiting Halifax and walking the Citadel), who he met (Ike Smith, future Premier of Nova Scotia) and how he felt leaving Mona at the train station, "did the children get to know me?". Marsh finally boarded a ship in Halifax on November 24 and arrived safe and sound after a rough crossing made better by having an upper bunk in a six-man cabin, each with their own sink and toilet.

On arrival in England on December 3, 1943 Marsh was posted through #1 CGRU (Canadian General Reinforcement Unit) and then spent almost two weeks at # 5 CIRU (Canadian Infantry Reinforcement Unit) close to London. During this period, he stayed at the New Norfolk Hotel, had lunch at the Canadian Club (Mrs. Vincent Massey was the hostess), Chesterfield Club, Royal Auto Club, Café Royal and visited a paper mill.

As his next appointment was not yet set he attended interviews with Colonel Chevrier and Brigadier Wolford. On December 11, he was appointed Staff Captain "Q" at Canadian Planning Staff, Canadian Military HQ, Canadian Army Overseas, in London. His third Christmas away from home was spent in London at a house party, at the Chesterfield Club (where he was staying and would leave his trunk for some time) and out on the town. On New Year's Day, he enjoyed a turkey dinner at the home of Mrs. Lloyd George (wife of the former British Prime Minister David Lloyd George).

---

[17] See Appendix 15 for Marsh's notes on "Principles of War" and enlargements of other printed/written memorabilia from the war years.

Canadian Planning Staff - HQ First Canadian Army

Back in Europe, settled in and ready for his next task, Marsh began his career at HQ 1st Canadian Army on January 4, 1944. Based in London, he began to work and socialize with many of the Canadian war correspondents that he would get to know very well when the war moved to the continent later that year. On January 3, he had tea at the home of Toronto Star reporter Paul Morton (who later in the war would become a controversial figure when he fired a Barretta pistol at a glass in a bar and was dropped behind enemy lines in Italy) and later in the month met well known Canadian

1st Canadian Army

Press reporter, Ross Munro at a pub. It was also during this period that Canadian officers were told to wear their ribbons so he begrudgingly wore his CVSM (Canadian Volunteer Service Medal), Silver Maple Leaf and chevrons on his tunic but lamented that they were, "getting as bad as the Americans!".

Telegram home advising of move to London

On January 15 Marsh received the wonderful surprise that he was going to be a father again, when he heard from Mona that she was pregnant with who would become John Marshall Irvine.

As part of the training for his role with the planning team Marsh attended a two-week course, "Joint Q Planning School", in London from January 17-31.

The class included American and British officers including his wife's cousin Ross McMaster, George Blackburn from Kentville, NS and a budding friendship with Lt. Col. Steve Cantlie (Black Watch Regiment of Canada) who would become famous in Canadian military history for his role in the disastrous battle of Verrieres Ridge (he was killed by a shell during the forming up for the battle on July 25 in Normandy with his command replacement leading the Black Watch up that ridge to their largest defeat in their history). During the course, the officers ate American rations (real sausage and tinned fruit!), socialized together (dances were organized with Jack Weir supplying the female companions from the WAAFS, WAACS and stenographer pools). It was during this time that some of the first flying bombs started to fall on London.

After the course was completed Marsh returned to his new job at Canadian Planning Staff, HQ 1st Canadian Army and the drudgery of the British winter. He was kept busy with his work and had time for socializing (dances, movies) and athletics including playing softball and soccer (General Montgomery had ordered that all ranks exercise between 2 and 4 pm every day). Letters note his happiness at Davie's hand-writing being "even and nice" and a curious double standard where Marsh laments that at home Mona is out in Cornwall going to parties. This theme comes up constantly in letters where Marsh seems less jealous (after all he was doing the same thing) but more furious at the able-bodied men of Cornwall who were at home dancing with his wife rather than being in the armed forces.

It was during February of 1944 that the infamous Canada vs. USA military football game took place in London (16-6 victory by Canada). Marsh missed the game as he was duty officer but he noted that it was like a McGill frat house after the game.

With promotion to Major very much on his mind, on February 17 Marsh was sent for three weeks as DAQMG (Deputy Assistant Quartermaster General) to work with HQ 3rd Canadian

EXTRACT from   PART II Orders   No 19, d/12 Feb 44
                    HQ First Cdn Army

                "C" CANADIAN PLANNING STAFF

26.   COMMAND:

      (a) On Command to 18th Joint Q Planning Course
           wef 0900 hours 17 Jan 44 to 0900 hours
           28 Jan 44.
           Major   W G SHAMBROOK
           Major   J W WEIR
           Captain A M IRVINE

      (b) On Command to HQ First Cdn Army wef 0900
           hours 31 Jan 44.
           Captain A M IRVINE.

      CERTIFIED true copy

                              (A I Matheson) Capt
                              Cdn Planning Staff.

Orders sending Marsh on course and then to First Canadian Army HQ

Infantry Division, his division and the home of the S, D and G's. He was moving around so much that he was having trouble getting his laundry done but he was very happy to be back in the division with so many old friends.

It was during his time with 3rd Division that they were visited and inspected by British General Bernard L. Montgomery. Simply by chance Marsh met "Monty" walking toward him and responded with a snappy salute to the future Field Marshall. Marsh moved back to the Plans Section of 1st Canadian Army on March 8 and prepared for his next posting which would be in a Liaison officer role with a different allied army HQ.

Prelude to the invasion – Second British Army and BUCO

On Loan to Second British Army

From March 22 to April 23 Marsh was loaned to HQ 2nd British Army to once again play an "Acting" DAQMG role.[18] He enjoyed the change very much as he had his best room to date in England, and enjoyed the British mess traditions of tea at 4:30 and dinner at 8:00 pm. Marsh wore his kilt to work on a regular basis, eliciting some stares from some but making him feel good about his connection to a Highland regiment in Canada. The Easter holiday was spent working as many of his friends went to Newcastle but he found time to go to the roof and watch the show put on by the searchlights and had tea at Mrs. Lloyd George's. Marsh reassured Mona that there were no other women (he specified blondes) in his life because, "the Yanks have a complete and absolute corner on the market".

2nd British Army

Playing a role in the planning for D-Day – on loan to BUCO (Build Up Control Organization) West

The period April 24 to June 3, 1944 was a time of excitement (Marsh's promotion to Major finally was approved), career challenge (being part of the final planning for D-Day) and disappointment (he developed pleurisy and was in hospital for the last two weeks of his posting to BUCO just before D-Day).

On April 24 Marsh was sent to Fort Southwick as Acting DAQMG as part of the ongoing Canadian team charged with planning the massive supply and build-up operation to support the Normandy landings now only a month away. It must have been an incredible place to be at that pivotal time in history. On May 5, his Majority was finally approved and his crowns were sewn on his tunic. A round of drinks was bought in the mess. With his Majority came the services of his first Batman, Herbert Clague, a young man from St. Boniface (suburb of Winnipeg) who would develop a long-lasting relationship with Marsh until the end of the war. Clague sewed on his crowns ("he did a good job"), did the wash for their officers (Marsh was asked to mark socks so the Batmen would not mix them up) and drove his jeep.

While at Fort Southwick Marsh visited the S, D and G's at the same time as General Eisenhower was addressing the regiment. Ike tried to visit every regiment that was to be involved in the initial assault prior to D-Day and the Canadians were no exception as the Canadian 3rd Division was to provide part of the assault troops for Juno Beach (North Nova Scotia Highlanders, North Shore Regiment and the S, D and G Highlanders). Marsh was delighted that a very fit looking 18th platoon all gathered around him to talk. There is no doubt that he likely felt somewhat melancholy about seeing his former men prepare for battle but there were much younger officers just as capable as he to lead them on June 6.

Sick with pleurisy and pneumonia

On May 17 Marsh's war took an unforeseen turn as many months of constant work and pressure took its toll and he fell ill and was sent to # 20 Canadian General Hospital with pleurisy and a touch of pneumonia.

---

[18] See Appendix 15 re: letter of commendation

He was very depressed that he was getting sick just as he was "getting someplace and making a real difference". One can only imagine the impact of this on a hard-working officer like Marsh who was in the thick of the D-Day planning. He got very depressed while in hospital as he saw years of training going to waste as he recovered. While in hospital he met many casualties from the Italian campaign, enjoyed real maple syrup, heard about many babies being born at home to his class-mates from # 7 CWSC but mostly lamented his bad luck to get sick at that moment in his career.

By June 1 he had recovered and due to the importance of his role at BUCO he had been replaced (the Colonel in charge of his section wanted him back but it was too late). Marsh therefore went back to HQ 1st Canadian Army in his Liaison role as a General Staff Officer II. With the invasion of France underway and knowing that he would soon make his way there with the HQ Liaison staff, Marsh got back to work and very quickly was feeling fit and strong again. Training was intensive within his section as they would eventually provide administrative support to the Liaison section attached to HQ 1st Canadian Army. His thoughts that June were both professional and personal as his third child was due to be born in early July. Baby names were thrown back and forth between he and Mona, both settling on John Marshall for a boy and Jennifer for a girl. As we now know John Marshall was born on July 3 (Marsh heard about by cable on July 5 as buzz bombs started to become a major concern in London) but the name Jennifer was kept alive when Marsh named his jeep "Jennifer" and his son David would have a daughter with that name, ironically born in 1970, the year that Marsh passed away.

On a somber note, Marsh was constantly scanning the casualty lists of the S, D and G Highlanders who were engaged in the fighting in France. He learned in June of the death of his good friend Archie MacDonald (noted in photo onboard the ship above) and asked Mona to send something to his widow.

France to Holland – Liaison Section – HQ First Canadian Army

Late July was spent in final preparations for debarkation to France, drawing rations, organizing vehicles and all the minutia of his Liaison Administration Section. Marsh was named a group commander for the move across the channel and finally boarded a Landing Ship Tank on July 24. The trip across the channel was smooth with good food and coffee reported. Landing in France on July 25 Marsh would not have known that that very morning six regiments of Canadian infantry and associated tanks and guns were engaged in one of the bloodiest and frustrating battles of the war just south of Caen, the battle of Verrieres Ridge. His friend Col. Steve Cantlie would play a tragic role in that battle as he was killed during the forming up period in May-sur-Orne. The Black Watch would be led up the ridge shortly after by Major Phil Griffin who was also killed and led that storied regiment to their worst losses of the war. Marsh did notice fighter planes heading for the battle when he finally landed and set up his office in a field behind Courseulles-sur-Mer.

Marsh made his way to the first of many headquarters of 1st Canadian Army just behind the beaches at Amblie. In their book, In the Footsteps of First Canadian Army, historians Angus Brown and Richard Gimblett wrote, "First Canadian Army

Armoured vehicles landing at Gold Beach

was the largest land formation ever formed and commanded in Canada and was twice as large as the Canadian Corps of the First World War. Logistically, it was responsible for feeding and maintaining hundreds of thousands of soldiers. Its challenge included tactical, operational, logistical and civil-military functions in a theatre characterized by joint and combined operations, heavily overlaid with diplomatic and domestic political responsibilities. Marsh would play a leading role in the liaison section that would help inform command decisions within First Canadian Army.

Marsh spent the next few weeks doing active liaison work that included visiting forward sections by jeep, bringing back information to Amblie including trips to Bayeax, Caen, Villers Bocage, Vire and St. Lo. In explaining the role of Liaison Officers in his book, Operational Handbook for the First Canadian Army 1944-1945, John Grodzinski noted, "The responsibilities of LO's included conveying the Command orders to subordinates (replacing the requirement for written orders, particularly when time was short); passing information to forward units and flanking formations; obtaining information from forward units; and maintaining physical contact with lower, higher or flank formations".

During this period, he visited the graves of his friends from the S, D and G's who were killed following D-Day in heavy fighting north of Caen. He drove hundreds of miles at night in his jeep named "Jennifer", enjoyed infrequent baths in a canvas tub and lived in a tent. He often told Mona that there was nothing to worry about but there is no question that from time to time he was close enough to the fighting to have been in danger from artillery and counter-attack. By the middle of August, the great break-out from Normandy was about to occur and Marsh would play a fascinating role in the Battle of the Falaise Gap.

Battle of the Falaise Gap – Earning a Mention in Dispatches honour

In mid-August, as the Canadian, Polish and American armies were advancing south of Caen, army commanders quickly realized that they were trapping a substantial number of German troops, tanks and guns. This was the remnants of the 5th Panzer and 7th German Army in France who were exhausted and trying to get over the Seine River to reorganize to fight another day.

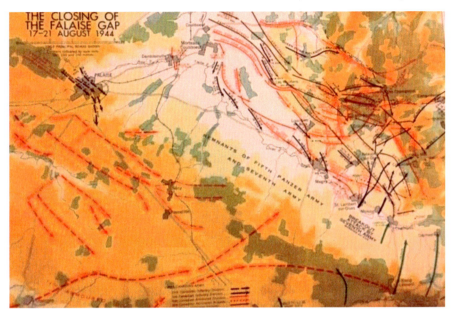

Closing of the Falaise Gap, France – August 1944

There was real concern on the part of First Canadian Army that their rapid advance could run into our American allies with potentially tragic results. For this reason, Marsh Irvine was sent on a special assignment by jeep and airplane to attempt direct liaison with General George Patton's Third US Army. The story of this mission will now be told for the first time.

On August 16 Marsh was given a short briefing by Brigadier Churchill Mann and handed a personal letter from General Crerar to General Patton. To find 3rd US Army now said to be near Fougeres, Marsh boarded an Auster spotter airplane and flew the route Amblie – Bayeux – St. Lo – Coutance – Granville – Avaranches – St. James – Fougeres – Laval – Le Mans. On the way they got lost numerous times, landed almost in the forward defence lines of a British unit, woke up some dozing GI's at Fourgeres and finally landed at Laval. After being advised that General Patton had moved on two days before Marsh presented his letter to First US Army and was promptly told that his services were not needed and that everything was in hand. With the plane already returned to Amblie Marsh set out to try to help First US Army until his communications truck arrived (it had been involved in a traffic accident with an American ammunition truck). They spent a night in a field north of Laval where one of his group became a casualty from a booby-trap and they had an encounter with German troops dressed in civilian clothing trying to escape. Marsh shared a tent that night with six French officers who slept in their clothing and boots, Marsh slept in his long underwear, just to be different.

After meeting with his communications truck and jeep they began the trip back to Amblie. On the way between Vire and Viller they came upon an area completely devastated and met the sole survivor of the village who, crazed from shock, was desperately searching for a bottle of cognac he had buried at the start of the war. Marsh and his team helped the man find his bottle and all helped the man celebrate his liberation.

The following observations have occurred to me and maybe of interest:

1) The idea of sending a liaison officer to Third U.S. Army apparently broke fast with no time to follow the usual Army channels of communication from Army to 21 Army Group to SHAEF and downward to Third U.S. Army. Undoubtedly by following the usual channels the reception given me by First U.S. Army would have been different from what it was.

2) Had Third U.S. Army been at LeMans and General Crerar's letter handed to General Patton my story might have been much different.

3) Had the signals vehicle arrived sooner, that is been despatched sooner and not been involved in an accident, some contribution to the cause might have been possible.

4) Looking back it would seem that SHAEF should have laid on direct liaison between the two Armies or better still, have put Third and/or First U.S. Army under command of 21 Army Group for the closing of the gap, as they must have had several days warning of the possible development of a pocket.

Marsh's conclusions on his abortive attempt to liase with Thrid US Army

Marsh would look back on his experiences during the closing of the Falaise Gap and conclude that had direct liaison been arranged and agreed upon at the highest command levels that the Gap would likely have been closed sooner with the result that many more thousand German troops and equipment may have been captured or destroyed.

By the KING'S Order the name of
Major A. M. Irvine,
General List, Canadian Army,
was published in the London Gazette on
21st June, 1945.
as mentioned in a Despatch for distinguished service.
I am charged to record
His Majesty's high appreciation.

Secretary of State for War

Certificate for being Mentioned in a Dispatch during Falaise Gap battle

For the role Marsh played in the action around the closing of the Falaise Gap he was awarded an oak leaf for being Mentioned in a Dispatch. Marsh noted in a letter on 15 April 1957 to historian C.P. Stacey that, "I have greatly enjoyed your writings so far and have been looking forward to the publication of the next volume (The Victory Campaign, published in 1960), which I am sure will make even more fascinating reading than its predecessors. The draft paragraphs are returned and I suggest that you leave well enough alone and not add to the already strained relations which seem to exist at present between Canada and the U.S.".

After the closing of the Falaise Gap the war in Normandy was all but over as the Germans were on the run and the allies were doing a full court press. Back at Main HQ Liaison section after his abortive attempt to liaise with the Americans, Marsh noted that the front was moving fast and he was unable to keep his maps up to date on an hourly basis. The Liaison section was also about to undergo a major change that would give Marsh a career opportunity to be the Officer Commanding a brand new Administrative Section.

Rear HQ – Administrative Liaison Section – Marsh gets to run his own show as Officer Commanding

On September 1, when the HQ was located at Brionne, Marsh would take on his biggest challenge of World War Two, Officer Commanding the Administrative Liaison Section at HQ, First Canadian Army. Being brand new, the unit had a different atmosphere, new mess and the officers and other ranks were all new to Marsh. At the beginning they had three jeeps, 1 x 160 # tent and joined # 13 Mess.

Battle honours - Liaison Admin - 1st Canadian Army

The section was responsible for delivering a daily morning conference for the senior officers of First Canadian Army (every day except Sunday) with information about operations during the preceding 24 hours. The ops summary included activities on the Canadian and all allied fronts. In his own words, "One or more members of the section work until well past midnight with the duty officer struggling to make chinagraph marks on talc to bring the ops maps up to the minute. Most of the sitreps were received between 2200 and 0800 hours and an early morning scramble in the cold was necessary to fill in the last details, scan the 1st Canadian Army Intelligence Summary and sift the wheat from the chaff of the Army Ops Logs". A total of 214 summaries were given from September 1, 1944 to May 7, 1945 by Marsh or someone from his staff, the last one taking place in a field between Hengelo and Enschede, Holland (map reference V3806).

The section moved along with main Liaison and the HQ staff which in September took them from Brionne to St. Mer Mesnil, Herbelle and Pihem until they moved into Belgium on September 19. As the battle was progressing everyone was working very hard but Marsh still had time to catch a movie, "Flesh and Fantasy", write plenty of letters home, enjoy some dulce that was sent by his mother, have a hot bath and enjoy their rum and beer ration. During this time Marsh got to watch up close the Battle of Boulogne and reported extensively to the Canadian Generals the progress and ultimate defeat of the British Airborne at Arnhem in Operation Market Garden. As it got colder in October they moved from tents to buildings.

Letters home at this time note more of the loneliness and minor jealousy that affected Marsh throughout the war, he made a special mention of his disfavour that Mona was out having fun at the Armoury dance in Cornwall and a special shot was made at the character of the men that she said were in attendance!

In October, they were on the move again entering Belgium, which Marsh noted was cleaner, neater and the towns and farms more prosperous than he had seen in France. For several days they were set up near the Chateau D'Oydonck near Deurle and went to Ghent for a mobile bath. Heavy fighting was occurring near Bergen Op Zoom and the Leopold Canal crossing that involved the S, D and G's so Marsh was constantly scanning the casualty lists to check on his old friends.

November was spent in Belgium in billets at the home of the "Fuch" family near Ghent. Marsh was busy working as the West Schelde and Maas battles took place close by and the Liaison section was rapidly growing with more Liaison Officer's and interpreters being added daily. He was elected to a three-month term as 13th Mess President which gave him the pleasure of sheets on a real bed as a perk of office which he enjoyed very much. All the men were focused on buying Christmas gifts for their families but prices were very high as the black market was rampant all over Europe.

Marsh relaxing, Nebo, Holland - April 1945

It was during this time that the manpower shortage was being felt by the infantry units and the Canadian government was frantically conscripting men to train and ship overseas to fight (they were given the nickname "Zombies" by those who had already volunteered). Marsh was not fond of the Zombies or of the "Westmount wives of officers overseas" who appeared to be having the time of their lives at home while their husbands were away.

Christmas Dinner

No. 13 Officers' Mess
HQ FIRST CDN ARMY

HOLLAND   25 December, 1944

By December most of the Canadian Army was settled into winter positions in Holland and HQ 1st Canadian Army was no exception. Marsh was stationed in Breda, Holland and spent time working (he lived in his office for some time), going to movies ("Forage Caps") and tried not to think of another Christmas away from home. Gifts arrived constantly from service clubs in Cornwall which helped the men though their

Hotel Cafe Rest. van Ham. Breda

No. 13 Mess, AJM HQ FIRST CDN ARMY, DEC 1944.

loneliness. Marsh received canned lobster and sardines in a package from Aunt Edna and a loving letter from Mona arrived just in time on Christmas eve. He worked late on December 24 and enjoyed his first eggs in two months on Christmas morning.

After working through the Christmas period, Marsh was excited to enjoy a 48 hour leave and went to Brussels on January 11. He stayed at the Atlanta Hotel (where his grandson Geoff would stay fifty years later), went to see the movie "Merry Widow" and enjoyed a night out with friends and three nurses for dinner and a dance (significant double standard at play as he went out and enjoyed himself while being unhappy that Mona was doing the same at home but that is most likely a sign of the times).

By late January First Canadian Army was busy preparing for Operation Veritable, the invasion of Germany and break-out from their winter positions. Marsh moved into a billet in the home of the "Beerker" family in Breda. He had been offered a new job to go to the plans section and was agonizing over what to do but ultimately with good advice from Jack Clunie decided not to take the move and stay in his OC position with his Liaison section. Operation Veritable, which started on February 8, would be the start of the final push to end the war and Marsh, while back of the actual fighting, was in the thick of it.

In his letters home, he often reassured Mona of this fact and also could be very funny. From a letter of February 22, 1945, "Jack Clunie returned from leave in UK today and looks 100 % better. His face is quite fat. We have had a busy time with the battle on but are a long way off from it and can just barely hear the guns

Rec Centre information, Nijmegan, Holland

when the wind is right".

On March 5 Marsh drove to Brussels and then took a train to Paris for a seven-day leave. He spent the week with Captain Al Eagles at the Hotel Savoy. They attended The Sadler's Wells ballet with Odile and Sabine St. Pierre from S. Aubin (near Dieppe) and also had lunch with their family, saw Glenn Miller and his orchestra, visited the palace at Versailles and generally relaxed, slept, read and enjoyed a hotel with clean sheets and hot baths. He debated buying gifts for his family or having a decent leave and the decent leave would win. Marsh would celebrate his 39th birthday on the way back to Grave, Holland where they were stationed on March 15, 1945.

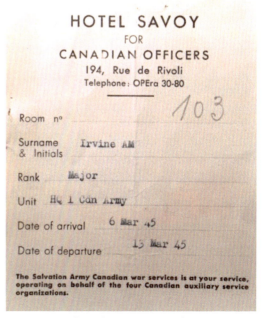

Leave in Paris, France - March 1945

Operation Varsity and the end of the war

On March 17, the final airborne landings of the war occurred when 1st Canadian Parachute Battalion jumped over the Rhine River. Marsh could watch the landings from a position in Wesel, Germany and noted to Mona in a letter of March 26, "It is looking mighty good honey". It was generally felt that crossing the Rhine was the last key natural barrier to the final push to defeat Germany and letters during this period show a much more upbeat and positive attitude from both Marsh and Mona. Marsh received his oak leaf for being Mentioned in a Dispatch during the Falaise Gap battle and was beginning to feel that he should do something new to prepare for the end of the war.

As the Spring brought warmer weather Administrative Liaison section once again moved to tents, "we are camped in a meadow near a small lake near a fine house, our mess is on the front lawn of this beautiful

place". They were near Delden, Holland and work continued to be busy but with the optimism that the war would end soon everyone had a jump in their step. Marsh was involved in a pool to guess what day of any given month that the war would end – he had the 4th. Marsh visited Emmerich, Germany and noted that the destruction was worse than he had noted in Caen, France. By late April Marsh had Liaison officers scattered throughout Holland (Groningen to Nijmegan, Apeldoorn to Almelo) trying to keep track of the fast-progressing final battles. Major cities in Germany were being captured along with senior German military leaders which made everyone hope that the end was very close. Marsh and his team were kept busy until well into the night reading "Views on the News" and the Army Ops Logs to ensure that their morning AQ Conference was comprehensive and up to date. They lived on hard tack and maple butter along with cocoa and scotch!

Marsh - Enschede, Holland - May 1945

As luck would have it Marsh was very close to winning the pool as a BBC flash announcement came over the radio on May 4 that all offensive action would cease and the Germans had agreed to surrender. Effective 0800 hours on May 5 the war would be over. The news was greeted by Marsh and his fellow officers and men as it was in most places, mostly by a solemn tear, a prayer for those who were lost and immediately thoughts turned to when they could all go home. Marsh gave a bottle of scotch that he had been saving to his boys and the terms of surrender were read out loud at the May 6 morning conference (although everyone looked rather sad that morning).

On May 9, the King spoke to all and every man felt proud to be part of the Commonwealth of nations who had finally beaten Germany. Marsh wrote in a letter home to Mona and the children, "at last you are going to have a daddy again". Initial indications about how long it would take to get home were set at October as everyone scrambled to figure out how many points they had. Marsh had 184 points based on 2 points/month of training in Canada, 3 points/month for each month overseas and 20 % bonus for being married.

Ops and Adm. Liaison dinner, Van Graf Hotel, Eschene, Holland – May 15, 1945

As the censorship of letters was removed as the war ended Marsh took the opportunity to tell Mona about some of the things that he would or could not while the war was in progress. Only then did she learn about a very close call that he had with a V2 bomb while in Antwerp and that he had lost 20 lb due to worry during the "baby blitz" in the UK during the winter of 1944. Marsh spent the next few months travelling throughout Holland visiting many of the cities they had liberated including a visit to an old Cornwall friend's aunt who he was informed had died four weeks before. On May 15, the Liaison section held a farewell banquet at the Van Graf Hotel in Enschede and Marsh went to The Hague in June for the Canadian Victory Parade. During these last months in Europe Marsh was stationed in Enschede and Apeldoorn and spent most of his working hours winding down the activities of the Liaison section. Every day more and more of his officers and men left to go home to Canada. There was much discussion back and forth between Mona, Marsh and Marsh's father about what Marsh should do. Marsh had been offered his old job back at the paper mill in Cornwall but there also was an option to volunteer for the Far East force or stay in the Army in some other capacity. Due to his expertise in logistics he was offered a position in the Far Eastern force and after some heavy soul searching agreed to take this position after having some time at home with his family. By July it was clear that the time to leave was coming soon and the remaining officers of First Canadian Army lined the road to cheer General Crerar as he left to return to Canada. It was during this event that Marsh spoke to General Guy Simmonds and reminded him that they had sat beside each other at Ashbury College but the good General did not remember!

Program for Liaison Section farewell dinner

Returning home to Canada

Marsh's last day in Holland was on July 30 when he boarded a Dakota plane to fly to England where he spent a week at # 1 Canadian Repatriation Depot. He was delighted to be in London with no bombs and promptly ordered a new suit at Jones, Chalk and Dawson and awaited debarkation orders. Marsh sailed home to Canada on August 11 on board the *DUCHESS OF RICHMOND* and arrived in Quebec City on August 17, two days after the Japanese surrender which meant immediate discharge from the army and a return to Cornwall and his family.

Back to the S, D and G's – Taking over command and post-war military life

Marsh as OC, S, D and G Highlanders

Marsh returned to Canada at the end of the summer of 1945 to a wonderful homecoming from Mona, Mona-Lou, David and new son John who he had never met. More military honours would come with the news that he would be awarded the Member of the Order of the British Empire and the Dutch decoration Order of Orange Nassau with crossed swords. Marsh stayed involved with the S, D and G's when the regiment reverted to being a reserve force unit. After being promoted to Lt. Colonel, Marsh was named Officer Commanding the regiment on November 1, 1949, a position he would hold until 1952. During this period the regiment would settle into a normal peacetime regime of activities including training, mess dinners, church parade, Remembrance Day, Men's Christmas Dinner, Officer's and Sergeant's turkey shoots and finally the New Year's Ball in both messes. Just prior to finishing his time as OC, Marsh had the proud honour to command the regiment during an inspection by General G.G. Simmonds when they were joined by cadets from Cornwall Collegiate and Vocational School that included his son, David Marshall Irvine.

Compiled and written by:
Geoffrey DePoint Irvine, Halifax, Nova Scotia
December 2016

A Brief Time Back in Canada

As mentioned in Geoff's narrative, in the spring of 1943, Captain Marsh Irvine returned to Canada to attend a Canadian War Staff Course at Royal Military College in Kingston, Ontario. He quickly located an apartment in the upper floor of a farm house owned by the Clarke Family at Collin's Bay, on Lake Ontario just outside Kingston, for Mum, Monie and me to stay in during his 6 months at RMC. He was on leave during most weekends, so we had a short opportunity to resume normal family life. It was during this period that John was conceived.

Dad and David

With the Clarke's help, we planted a garden that involved the combined efforts of our whole family.

Monie made friends with Frances, the Clarke's daughter, while I made friends with David Sinclair, who lived next door with his family. While we were there we shared that family's grief when David's father, a professor at Queen's University in Kingston, drowned while swimming in the Lake in front of their house. I have kept in touch with David over the years, as we played football against each other in high school, until this day when he is now a retired Anglican Minister living in the Laurentians. David and his wife, Georgia, who is also a minister, visited us at Quince Cottage a few years ago.

During Dad's time overseas, he and Mum corresponded continually. Mum's letters to him have been lost, but a great many of Dad's have been saved and have been preserved by Geoff in binders for easy access. He plans to digitize all the letters as time permits.

Dad never forgot our special days and usually sent a book as a gift. My special favourite was "The Flying Scotsman" and I think Monie's would have been "Madeline", both of which have been enjoyed by our children and grandchildren. Postcards came our way any time he was on leave, as well as letters addressed to us separately.

John Marshall Irvine was born the third of July 1944 in the Cornwall General Hospital.

Post-war Years

While Dad was overseas, Mum rented various St. Lawrence River summer cottages at Stonehouse Point, Sheek Island and Kamp Killkare at Aultsville, which was where we were when Dad arrived home in August 1945. Rent that year and for a number of years after, as we continued to rent the same cottage, was $75.00 for the month This included furniture, hydro and ice for the ice-box plus a flat bottomed, wooden, Verchere row boat. We had to supply our own linen and cutlery! I can recall sitting together on the steps

Stonehouse Point Cottage

of the Aultsville cottage, soon after Dad's arrival home, while he carved several small boats for me to play with in the River. In later years, I could take the row boat out alone as long as I stayed within sight of the cottage. During these times Michael Gray and I would sail the fully rigged, two-foot-long sailboat that Grandpa Irvine had been given by Lord Strathcona, when Grandpa retired from the Hudson's Bay Company. Donald Alexander Smith, later named 1st Baron of Strathcona and Mount Royal was, among other illustrious pursuits, a long-time employee and President of the Hudson's Bay Company.

Most summers while Dad was away, we would either join in a rental with, or rent adjacent to, Mum's good friend Margie Gray and son Michael. Captain Bob Gray and Dad had become best friends in the Regiment and went overseas together. At Aultsville, Auntie Marg, (as we then called her) and Michael were in the cottage next door and one of the main reasons why we rented at Stonehouse Point was that the Gray's, including daughter Debbie by that time, rented a cottage one over form ours. The Philip Woolcombe family of Montreal were in between.

In early 1950, we rented from the Craibe family a rather basic cottage at Stonehouse Point, which was enjoyed by the family every summer until 1963. The Craibe family, who had a son in Monies's class and a daughter in mine lived in Glen Walter, where we went for groceries, ice cream cones and gas for the outboard motor. The cottage sat on the bank of the St. Lawrence River, about 8 miles east of Cornwall and about 30 feet from the water and John recalls the rent being $300.00 a month. Non-drinking water was pumped from the river with a hand pump that Dad and John installed in the kitchen.

Irvine family at Stonehouse Point

The outhouse was "out back". Each year a local fellow would show up in the spring and ask if we wanted to be "done up out back". This entailed digging a new pit and moving the outhouse over onto it!

The River was our bathtub and every morning about 6am Dad would be in the water having his bath before going to work. Some mornings in early and late summer it was chilly.

Stonehouse Point derived its name from the ruins of an historic stone house that was on the property and viewed as one traversed the long roadway leading to the many cottages.[19]

Mona Lou's husband, Phil Webb, proposed to Monie at the base of the ruins of the old stone house. Since Phil was quite a talented artist, he later produced a painting of the ruins to memorialize the site and the event.

Some time before that John recalls Monie bringing a previous beau named Gordon Mesley, to the cottage for at least one visit. John further recalls that Mum and Dad were not impressed with Mr. Mesley, whose daughter Wendy, now reads the CBC National News.

John's fond recollections of the Stonehouse Point years include having peeing contests with Michael and Christopher Morris and Brooks Giles, sitting on the peak of the roof of the Giles boathouse to see who could pee over the edge first; gathering old cigarette butts from their parents to smoke in pipes made from hollowed out acorns with stems of hollow reeds; and finally trying out my new Corvair and driving it into the River. Good stuff!

Marshall back on civvy street at HSPM

Jumping over Dad's life overseas, we can pick him up back on "civvy street" adjusting to being back at work at Howard Smith Paper Mills in his old job of Office Manager on October 30, 1945, while at the same time adjusting to family life with a wife and three children. I had no appreciation at the time, nor do I have to this day, of what he and Mum were going through during those early years back home, and likewise what I was going through to be displaced as the "man of the house". No doubt my nose was out of joint, but I hope it was offset by the pleasure of having my father back home.

Whether it was because he was trying to make up for lost time, or just that same acute sense

---

[19] See Appendix 16 for picture and informnation on Stonehouse Point Historic Site

of duty that he learned from his parents and that prompted him to enlist before the war, Dad immediately took on a great many community activities in addition to his demanding full-time work. Not wanting to cut his ties with the Regiment with which he began his military career, he remained in the S.D.&G Highlanders Militia for 6 more years, during which he commanded the Regiment from 1949 to 1952, with the rank of Lieutenant Colonel. Involvement with the Regiment included an active Mess social life. St. Andrews Day and New Years Eve were celebrated by formal balls and these plus Mess dinners gave Dad an opportunity to invite some of his former superiors from overseas to be guests of honour. These included most of the important senior Canadian officers from WWII including Generals H.D.G. (Harry) Crearer, Guy Simmonds, F.F. Worthington, E.L.M. Burns, Charles Foulkes, Chris Vokes and Michael Knight. Special civilian guests included local MP Lionel Chevrier, and Col. Jack Franklin, at that time Sergeant-At-Arms in the House of Commons. I was privileged to meet many of them, as

Lt.Col. Irvine in dress blues.

Mum and Dad usually entertained them and their wives at a cocktail party before the event.

At retirement in 1952 Dad was offered a full-time job with a Regional Command and a promotion to Brigadier-General, but he had finally had enough of the military and turned it down.

Mona and Marsh after MBE investiture

Soon after returning home Dad was presented with the two most important decorations he had been awarded during the war. At an investiture at the Dutch Embassy in Ottawa with Mum and his parents in attendance, he was declared an Officer of the Order of Orange Nassau with Swords by Prince Bernhard of the Netherlands. Later at an investiture for area recipients of decorations, held at the Athletic Grounds opposite the Armories in Cornwall, Dad was inducted into the Order of the British Empire as a Member (MBE) by the then Governor General of Canada, Viscount Alexander of Tunis.[20] Other acknowledgments of his contribution came during the war when he was twice Mentioned in Dispatches.

In the latter years of 1940s, he Chaired the Stormont County Citizen's Rehabilitation Committee, formed to find housing and provide assistance of all kinds to returning veterans, Chaired the Canadian Legion Branch 297 and served on the Trustees for some years after.

---

[20] See Appendix 15 for copy of MBE Citation

During the 1950's he organized and was first President of Cornwall Branch of the Canadian Cancer Society, then remained active in the Society for another 10 years. He was instrumental in developing the S.D.& G. Highlanders military museum in the Cornwall Armories, was active in the First Battalion Highlanders Officer's Association, and was named a Life Member of the S.D.& G. Highlanders Officers Mess.

In the field of education, Dad was elected for a number of terms to the Cornwall Public School Board, where he served as an Officer and member of the Finance and Public Relations Committees and was elected Chairman of the Board in 1960. Also in 1960, he Co-Chaired the Cornwall YMCA Property Committee, during the purchase of land to build a new Y on Fifth Street East.

Active as a member of the Executive of the Stormont, Dundas and Glengarry Historical Society, Dad helped establish the United Counties Museum in the former Wood Family House in west end Cornwall, and was then named one of the Governors of the Museum. He was also a member of the executive on the board of the Cornwall Branch of the Canadian Red Cross Society.

From a business standpoint, Dad was a member of the Industrial Cost Accountants Societies of both Ontario and Quebec, the Technical Section of the Canadian Pulp and Paper Association, the Canadian Manufacturer's Association and the American Management Association, as well as being a Commissioner of Oaths in both Ontario and Quebec.

I believe both Dad and Grandpa Irvine maintained detailed financial ledgers throughout their lives, but unfortunately the only one I have of Grandpa Irvine's begins in 1942, while Dad's begins after the war in 1946. They make interesting reading and earlier copies might have revealed more history that has been lost.

In case anyone might think that Dad never had any fun, he was a long time Member of both the SD&G Badminton Club and the Cornwall Golf and Country Club and loved swimming and fishing. I think some of his favourite leisure hours were spent in one of our several motor boats fishing for hours with his best friend, Bob Gray, on the St. Lawrence River. He also loved fly- fishing and was usually invited once a year by his working colleague and friend, Newton Candee, to a fishing camp on the Que'vion River in Quebec, north of Ottawa.

Regarding the SD&G Badminton Club, it was where the whole family played at the Armories at one time or another. Monie and I belonged to the Junior Club, where we played on Saturdays in the winter and competed for medals at the end of the season. I believe I still have a few in a box somewhere.

In 1949, after living on York Street for sixteen years, the family purchased the stately, red-brick house at 39 Fouth Street East in Cornwall, from the Eatons who lived next door. Built originally as the Cornwall Grammar School in 1855, where the teachers lived upstairs over the classrooms, the house required considerable renovations before we moved in and continued to receive many DIY projects from Dad and his sons over the years until 1963. Some years after Mum and Dad had moved, the house at 39 Fourth was named a Provincial Heritage Building

39 4th Street East, Cornwall

Whether it was fostered during his school days at Ashbury, developed during his military career or was handed down from his very fastidious father, Dad was always a "well turned out" gentleman. Suit, shirt and tie and well shined shoes were his normal work day and Sunday dress. Every Sunday when the weather was fit, the whole family would walk down two blocks on Sydney Street to Knox United Church. At most times, in addition to Sunday, Dad wore a fedora hat, which he lifted and bowed his head any time we met a lady or entered a building. If he was still alive, he would be appalled to see a great many boys and men of today wearing baseball caps indoors and even at the table in restaurants.

Douglas Marshall Irvine was born May 31, 1952 at Cornwall General Hospital.

For many years, before and after the war, Dad was Office Manager of the Cornwall Division of Howard Smith Paper which later became Domtar Limited. In 1957, Dad was promoted to Administrative Officer of the Domtar Research Laboratory in Cornwall. This was in preparation for a further move in 1962 to a newly built Domtar Research Centre in Senneville, Quebec, on the western end of Montreal Island. This entailed an additional promotion to Divisional as well as Research Centre Administrative Officer.

Cornwall First Baptist Church was the scene in February 1962 of the joining in marriage of Sylvia Jean Smith and David Marshall Irvine, with a quiet reception afterward at Sylvia's parent's home at 627 Gloucester Street.

In 1963 the Irvines purchased a cottage at Hamilton's Island, 15 miles east of Cornwall near Summerstown, for $7,000.00, which was sold in 1976 for $13,500.00. Still on the St. Lawrence River, but a bit further back from the water, it was a much more finished building with pressurized water in the kitchen and bathroom drawn by electrical pump from the River. Since I had left home by '63, I have little recollection of the cottage, but do remember a "bunkie" being built at the back by Hodgins Lumber soon after the purchase. Due to the steep bank and the amount of wash from passing freighters, Dad's boat was kept in a boathouse on the back side of the Island, near the bridge to the mainland. For easier access, from time to time, it was hung from two weeping willow trees immediately in front of the cottage, like the davits on a ship.

Fairfield

Interestingly, Summerstown was where our Great Grandfather Captain John Andrew McMaster purchased "Fairfield" as a summer home in 1900. Fairfield was partly a retirement house and partly a project for his nephew, Barry Clark from the Isle of Man, who John Andrew was helping become a farmer. It was a very grand brick house with a farm and large acreage that was built by the famous John A. (Cariboo) Cameron in 1865. Cameron had grown up in Summerstown and returned to build the house after making his fortune in the British Columbia gold fields in 1863. The house remained in the McMaster family until 1917, when Grandfather Andrew McMaster decided to run as a Laurier Liberal in the County of Brome in Quebec and a new, only slightly less grand, property was developed near Knowlton, Quebec. Mum had spent many summers at Fairfield with her large family as a young girl and recalled trips in the motor boat, buggy rides, Mr. Guindon the gardener and sneaking up to the cupola on the roof to secretly sew, knit and play cards, which were all forbidden on Sunday. While I was still at home the house was purchased by the Catholic Church and with additions was renovated into a seminary.

706 Dowker Drive in Baie d'Urfe'

In the summer of 1963 Dad, Mum, John and Doug moved to a very attractive and comfortable, Quebec style, stone house at 706 Dowker Drive in Baie d'Urfe', a long-established West Montreal Island subdivision located between Pointe Claire and Ste. Anne de Bellevue. Situated on the edge of the campus of MacDonald College, this was "deja' vu all over again", as Dad had summered as a boy at Beaurepaire just down the road and they had first met at MacDonald College in the summer of 1926 while Mum trained for her teaching certificate and Dad did his McGill surveying.

Coincidentally, Sylvia and I moved to Ste. Anne de Bellevue from Blind River in 1963, as I had accepted the position as Secretary-Manager of the Canadian Institute of Forestry, with my office being in the basement of the

Ladies' Residence at MacDonald College. We purchased an old house at 16 Perrault Avenue in Ste. Annes, so could spend lots of time with the rest of the family.

By then John was at Queen`s University in Kingston and Doug was at Dorset Elementary School.

Although living in a new community, for Mum and Dad it was like coming home to renew friendships with childhood friends and relatives and to make many new friends. They and we joined Union United Church in Ste. Anne de Bellevue, where Dad chaired the Board of Stewards and Mum became active in the W.M.S.. Dad served as Membership Chairman of the Baie d'Urfe' Citizens' Association, while Mum enjoyed volunteering and meeting friends at a community-run tea room in Ste. Anne de Bellevue, called Au Petite Café.

Summers were spent at Hamilton's Island, to which Dad very often commuted when not on holidays.

In the Fall of 1967 Dad was hospitalized and operated on for what turned out to be a precursor to his later cancer. The surgeons believed that they had removed it all, but that was not to be.

Marshall at his retirement party - 1969

In the spring of 1969 Dad took early retirement due to ill health and he and Mum moved back to Cornwall to the newly purchased home at 512 James Street in Riverdale, a post-war sub-division at the western end of the City. They had maintained contact with many of their Cornwall friends, so they re-connected very seamlessly and moved back into the life of Knox United Church.

On the 3rd of March 1970, Mum and Dad's 39th anniversary, Dad was checked in to Queen Elizabeth Hospital in Montreal for observation to determine the cause of stomach pains. After three days of tests that showed only some small stones in the gallbladder, Dad was operated on and in his words, "some adhesions removed and some piping rerouted"!

By the 6th, of April, with pain continuing and x-rays showing a probable kink in his intestine, Dad was operated on again, but experienced little improvement.

By the 21st, what Dad had feared was confirmed, that malignant matter had also been removed. On the 22nd, after his surgeon, Dr. Lloyd Smith, had consulted with Mum and Dad, his diary entry read, "I may have one year to go! Considerable thought will have to be given to the plans for the future".

A third operation was carried out on the 7th of May, which appeared to improve the situation so that he was able to return home on the 27th of May after eighty-five days in hospital. He weighed 125 pounds, but enjoyed an ounce of scotch with his sleeping pill that first night home.

At some point when I was quite young Dad showed me a small stamp album that he was given as a boy. We began to collect stamps together and for Christmas 1946, when I was eleven, Mum and Dad gave me a stamp album of my own. Until I left home we collected and put stamps in my album, although at some point along the way Dad acquired another bigger loose-leaf album of his own that he continued to use. I think it is probably rare to have a hobby that follows you from youth to the grave, but that is what Dad had in his stamp collecting, which is proven by his daily diary entries during 1970 with the last entry being November 6th. Although I know he considered it fun to "mess around" with stamps, he always referred to it, right to the end, as "working on stamps"!

While his time in hospital was anything but pleasant health wise, it did give Dad an opportunity to spend quality time with many Montreal friends and relatives, particularly his brother Laurie, who spent countless hours at his bedside. It was very hard on Mum, who traveled to Montreal alone by train, or with friends or John and Doug on a continual basis and very often stayed over for varying periods with old friends and relatives.

Back home during the early days of spring 1970 he could go for lengthy walks, get out to visit friends, do some flower and shrub gardening and plant two tomato plants. But as the summer progressed so did his cancer, with the result that by early fall he spent more time on the rester out on the porch and lawn or in bed on heavier doses of medication. Dr. Lorne Caldwell, who had been Dad's doctor for many, many years, visited the house very often offering support and closely monitoring Dad's medication.

Dad's diary entries, while mostly upbeat as he identifies all his many visitors, sometimes showed his frustration at what he was going through. On September 21st he wrote, "Feel my time is getting short and do not want to go as I have so much to live for". Again, on the 22nd he wrote, "Feeling pretty rocky and bloated. Unhappy about my deteriorating condition". Then on a happier note he reported that his two tomato plants had produced 100 tomatoes!

On November 7th John met Sylvia, Geoff, Jennifer and me at Montreal West Station and drove us to Cornwall for a ten day visit to Upper Canada. Near the end of our stay we borrowed Dad's car and drove to Toronto to visit the Webbs for three days. While in Cornwall Dad and I talked each day and Dad wrote in his diary, "Wonderful to have him to talk to. A real tonic. We talk the same language due to his efforts and experience. Only sorry he is just staying a week". Then on the last day, after we had left he wrote," Have a feeling I will not see them again. Gave Dave my father's gold pocket watch, chain and pencil".

Inside the back cover of the watch is engraved: "Arthur M. Irvine from his parents on his 21st Birthday July 12th 1902 - MICAH.VI.8". This verse reads: "He hath shewed thee, O man, what is good; and what doth the Lord require of thee, but to do justly, and to love mercy, and to walk humbly with thy God".

These items I cherish and carry in my vest pocket on special occasions, while thinking that I do not believe there is any question that Marshall Irvine lived up to his parent's expectations.

Although we both knew it would be our last time together, I will regret forever that we did not acknowledge that fact and say the things that should have been said including, "I love you", plus hug instead of shaking hands, for what would have been the first time since before I was a teenager.

Dad could keep his own diary entries until half way through December 6th, when Mum took over. She wrote "no visitors wanted", on December 8th and on the 9th that "Dad was taken by ambulance and admitted to the Cornwall General Hospital in very weak condition". Mum spent all day and night on the 10th at the Hospital and while she was at home for a short sleep, Dad passed away mid-day on the 11th. He was 64 years old.

The body was handled by McArthur Bros.& MacNeil Funeral Home in Cornwall with a closed casket visitation followed by transferral to Montreal for cremation, where a family service of committal was held at Mount Royal Cemetery Crematorium. Burial was in the family plot with his parents on a hillside in Mount Royal Cemetery. A memorial service was held at Knox United Church at a later date.

"Loss To The Community", was the title of an editorial in the *Cornwall Standard Freeholder* on December 19th,1970, that read as follows: "Cornwall lost a well-known citizen last week when A. Marshall Irvine died after a lengthy illness. Citizens paid tribute to his memory at a memorial service this week and no tribute was greater deserved for Marshall Irvine was a fine, sincere, community-minded citizen, highly respected as a gentleman, for his business integrity, and also for his distinguished military career".[21]

But Dad's exemplary life lives on in his children and grandchildren, plus great grandchildren, and now great, great grandchildren, that unfortunately he never knew.

Brass plaque on Irvine family gravestone

---

[21] See Appendix 17 for newspaper articles

Margaret Mona (McMaster) Irvine (1908 – 1999)

The story of my Mum's life has been inextricably woven throughout the previous narrative of Dad's life, but she deserves to be recognized individually. The immensely meaningful contribution she made to the lives of her husband and us four children can never be covered adequately in any form. However, the following eulogy given by our brother, John Marshall Irvine, as a Celebration of her life at her funeral on February 28th, 1999, tells you something about the person she was.

Each of us present today brings to this celebration of life our own personal memories and our own unique perspective of Mum and how she touched our lives. To Mona Lou, David, Douglas and I, she was "Mum"; to Frankie, Bunny, Amelia, John and Helen, she was "sister Mona"; to all of her grandchildren and great grandchildren she was "Gram-i"; to nephews and nieces and several close family friends she was "Auntie Mona"; to those of you who were close to her as a friend she was "Mona"; and finally, to those of you who perhaps knew her through her offspring, she was "Mrs. Irvine". This afternoon, I would like to share with you, on behalf of my sister and brothers, a little of Mum's life and the memories we have of her. I hope that some of my words may recall a happy memory for you too.

Margaret Mona (McMaster) Irvine

Mum was born in Montreal in 1908. Along with her four sisters and brother she was part of a very politically active family. Her Dad, Andrew Ross McMaster, served as a Member of Parliament in Ottawa and later as a cabinet minister in the Quebec Legislature. No doubt this exposure to civic life was partly responsible for the active role that Mum took in the life of her community. After her marriage to Arthur Marshall Irvine in 1931, and the birth of their first child Mona Lou in 1933, the young family moved to Cornwall in 1935. Except for a six-year period from 1963 to 1969, when she and Dad lived in Baie D'Urfee, Mum has been a resident of Cornwall.

Family, Church and Community were the focal points of Mum's life. Of these her husband and her children were of prime importance, as evidenced by the fact that she spent almost 40 years with at least one child at home. During these forty years she experienced the Great Depression, Dad's absence during World War II, and all of the usual childhood illnesses.

We especially remember her exceptional cooking and baking talents. Our Sunday dinners with homemade ice cream and chocolate sauce or my favourite, apple crisp. The evening meal was always served in the dining room with all family members present. Although we were not a family who communicated with each other a lot, a great deal of who we are and what we stand for was passed to us by Mum's modelling of appropriate behaviour and her strong moral values. We find it difficult to remember a time when Mum ever raised her voice or spoke harshly to one of us. I'm sure there were times when we deserved it, especially after that forbidden trip to Massena or St.

Zotique!! When she did let us know that she was upset or displeased it was always in a quiet and calm manner.

Mum loved life and her positive attitude, her friendly smile and outgoing personality, endeared her to almost everyone with whom she came into contact. During her active years she rarely missed a Sunday service at Knox United Church and then Knox-St. Paul's. She served as a Sunday School teacher, she helped to organize the first Friendship Circle (the beginnings of the United Church Women), she was President of the UCW and took a leadership role in her church group. I remember many a lemon meringue pie or batch of cookies that found a spot at some Church Bazaar, Tea or dinner instead of in our tummies!! If you were a visitor or new member to our congregation, Mum would have welcomed you with warm and friendly words. Her Christian faith served as a foundation for all that she did and her life was a model of Christian upbringing.

Mum lived and enjoyed a very active life up until about 7 years ago. She played golf, skied cross-country, swam, dove and even on occasion, kicked a soccer ball with her grandchildren. Any of her grandchildren, who were old enough before her decline, are experts at Casino, Snap, Fish and Old Maid. One of her favourite passions was to watch athletics on television. CFL or NFL football, Hockey Night in Canada, golf and tennis tournaments all earned her avid attention. In her retirement years, Mum enjoyed spirited games of bridge with a wide circle of friends. Although she never mastered the intricacies of the game, she did derive a great deal of enjoyment from the camaraderie that it provided.

Mum's active life was also a benefit to her community. If you were new to her neighbourhood she would be the first at your door to welcome you with a warm smile and a plate of cookies or a pan of squares. She developed many lasting friendships with her neighbours wherever she lived. The Canadian Cancer Society was Mum's favourite charity and she served in many voluntary roles: as Service to Patients Chairman, Area Captain for the door-to-door canvass, a tagger on tag day and for many years as a greeter at the Cancer Clinic at the General Hospital. During her life, she made valuable contributions of her time and talents to The Canadian Red Cross, The Heart and Stroke Foundation, Meals-on-Wheels and the Auxiliary of the Cornwall General Hospital, often working in the Tuck Shop.

Whether it was the effort that made a birthday party the best ever, the bonding time you had while drying dishes at the kitchen sink, or the warm welcome received by your friends, the common ingredient was Mum. We mourn her death but we cherish and celebrate the memories *that* we each have of her time with us. May God be with her.

For more detailed information on Mona McMaster see A Family Story, written by Mum's sister Helen for their sister Frankie's 80th Birthday. (Available from the Author.)

SIXTH TO NINTH GENERATIONS

Mona Louise (Irvine) Webb (1933) *(John, John, John Edward, Arthur Marshall, Arthur Marshall)*

Mona Louise (Irvine) Webb

Mona Louise, only daughter of Mona and Marshall was born February 22nd, 1933 in Montreal, moving three months later to Cornwall, Ontario. She attended Miss Jack's Kindergarten, Cornwall Public School and Cornwall Collegiate and Vocational School. High school activities included socializing, Students' Council, organizing volleyball and badminton, cadets, assistant editor of CCVS year book and teaching Sunday School.

Her ambition to become a teacher took her to Queen's University, followed by a summer pre-teachers course in Toronto and a year teaching kindergarten in Cornwall and Ottawa Teachers' College, followed by 2 years teaching in Kingston and an additional 3 years of teaching in Toronto.

One summer she toured Europe with 3 friends.

While teaching she met and married Philip John Webb of Toronto, a generous, kind, amusing, loving, sports car enthusiast and later committed, affectionate dad and grandfather. Living in Don Mills, Ontario from 1967 – '88, they spent their summers visiting David and Sylvia in Nova Scotia and assisting with the operation of Harbourview Inn. The lure of inn keeping culminated in the purchase of Harbourview Inn at Smith's Cove in 1980 and began 20 years of winters in Toronto and summers in Nova Scotia. A family business, with Marshall gardener/cook, Peter waiter, Andrea star waitress, Philip historical host and bartender and Mona Lou chief cook and hostess. With the sale of the Inn in 2000 and their children launched, they began a retirement of travel in the winter and summers in Nova Scotia.

Mona, (Monie to brother John and school friends, Moe to Philip and brother David, Lou to brother Doug and Grandma and Mona to her grandchildren) a widow since 2010, continues to live an active life. A long-time member of the United Church of Canada and U.C Women at Bethedsa in Don Mills and Roncesvalles; exercise classes; pursuing her hobby of rug hooking; driving her grandsons to hockey and lacrosse and visiting family and friends.

Mona Lou was married to Philip John Webb (1930-2010) of Toronto at Knox United Church on the 6th of August 1960. They have Philip Marshall Webb (1962), Peter Livingstone Webb (1966), and Andrea Lynn Webb (1969). Marshall is unmarried as at 2017. He has a daughter Dakota Fletcher (1994). Peter Webb married (1st) Kristen Lee Duffy (1966) in 1990 and they had Peter Livingstone Webb Jr. (1996) and Kendall Mahew Webb (1999). Peter married (2nd) Denise Irene Garcia (1969) in 2007. Andrea Webb married Bradley Alexander MacDonell (1969) in 2000 and they have Aiden Alexander MacDonnell (2003) and Angus John MacDonnell (2005).

David Marshall Irvine (1935) *(John, John, John Edward, Arthur Marshall, Arthur Marshall)*

David Marshall Irvine

David was born to Mona and Marshall Irvine on the 11th of November 1935 at the Cornwall General Hospital in Cornwall, Ontario, Canada. Cornwall's Central Public School provided his elementary education, followed by graduation from Cornwall Collegiate and Vocational School. In high school, he competed on the track and football teams; filled various positions on the Student Council along with being a King Scout, a camp counselor and active in the YMCA, from Gra-Y to Hi-Y to Y-teens. In his final year, he attained the rank of Lt. Col. as Commanding Officer of the CCVS's entire school cadet corps.

Proceeding to the University of New Brunswick, he was a halfback on the UNB Red Bombers, ran with the track team and served on the Student Council before graduating with a Bachelor of Science in Forestry in 1959. During his summers, he worked in forestry positions for various paper companies in Northern Quebec, Northern Ontario and Cornwall and for the Alberta Forest Service. In the fall of 1959 he traveled abroad and spent eight months visiting most of western Europe, the British Isles, Scandinavia and North Africa. Upon his return to Canada he worked for several different Woodlands Divisions of Domtar Ltd in northern Ontario and qualified as a Registered Professional Forester. In 1962, he married his high school sweetheart Sylvia Jean Smith (1938) of Cornwall, a Registered Nurse, and very soon afterward accepted the position of Secretary-Manager of the Canadian Institute of Forestry at Macdonald College on the western end of Montreal Island in Ste. Anne de Bellevue, Quebec. Geoffrey DePoint Irvine was born in 1965 at the Lakeshore General Hospital in nearby Pointe Claire.

Seeking a new challenge, in 1967 the Irvines purchased Harbour View House and Cottages, a summer resort with a long and storied history in the province of David's ancestors at Smith's Cove, Digby County, Nova Scotia. Jennifer Roope Irvine was born in 1970 at the nearby Digby General Hospital.

Now, after 50 years in Nova Scotia, they can look back with pride at what they have accomplished. The 75-acre Harbour View property is now a thriving community containing over 30 privately owned seasonal cottages and year-round homes, the remodeled Harbour View Dance Casino, in which they reside with plenty of room for visiting family and friends, plus the popular Harbour View Inn.

Throughout their time in Nova Scotia, both Sylvia and David have been very active in their immediate community and the wider communities that surround them in the fields of health and safety, economic development, religion, municipal government, heritage, tourism, adult education, recreation and the environment. Both have received The Danny Gallivan Volunteer Award, while David has also received The Queen's Golden Jubilee and Fire Services Exemplary Service Medals, in addition to receiving an Honorary Diploma from the Nova Scotia Community College. At 81 years of age, David continues to be involved in a number of committees in the local area, while pursuing his passion for genealogical research and keeping in touch with friends near and far on the Internet.

David Marshall Irvine (1935) married Sylvia Jean Smith (1938) at Cornwall First Baptist Church on February 10, 1962. They have Geoffrey Depoint Irvine and Jennifer Roope Irvine.

Geoffrey DePoint Irvine (1965) married Kelly Lynn MacDonald in 1991 and they have Williston James Marshall Irvine (1994), whose partner is Sophia Magdalen Eileen Rumball Geraci (1995), Julia MacDonald Irvine (1996) and Georgia Margaret Irvine (2001). Kelly and Geoff are divorced. Geoffrey's partner is Julie Anne Toman (1968)

Jennifer Roope Irvine (1970) married Robert Edward Begrand in 1994 and they have Oliver Robert Benz Begrand (1998) and Benjamin David Begrand (1999). Jennifer and Rob are divorced. Oliver is the father, with Faith Wilson, of Harrison Robert James Begrand (2016). Jennifer's partner is James Warren Reid (1956).

John Marshall Irvine (1944) *(John, John, John Edward, Arthur Marshall, Arthur Marshall)*

John Marshall Irvine

Second son of Mona and Marshall Irvine, John was born July 3rd, 1944 during World War II, so did not meet his father until he was 13 months old.

During his days at Central Public School, kick-the-can, shinny hockey in the driveway, tag football, hop scotch and skipping were early activities. During the winter, he spent endless hours playing shinny hockey on the rink at Central Public.

John attended Cornwall Collegiate and Vocational School where he played Jr and Sr Basketball and earned a trip to the All Ontario Golden Ball Tournament in 1963. He played tackle football both 8-man and then Senior. In his final year, he was captain of the team. John also participated in cadets like his sister and older brother.

In 1961, with summer jobs scarce, he traveled to Holland, England, France, Switzerland and Italy as part of Stewart's French Language Tour to Europe.

After high school, he entered Queen's University. Two highlights of John's two full-time years were playing varsity football for the Golden Gaels and flunking out after his second year! Ten years later he received his BA from Queen's. He later added B. Ed. and M. Ed. degrees from Ottawa U.

In 1965, John moved back home to Baie d'Urfe'. He worked at General Motors as a parts picker, skied every weekend in the Laurentians and took a course at Sir George Williams (Concordia) U.

After a year at Ottawa Teachers' College, John was hired by the Etobicoke Board of Education (now part of Toronto). He spent three years in Etobicoke before returning to Cornwall, and a three-year teaching post at Longue Sault Public School, where he met his first wife Mary Heather (Dewar) Harland and her daughter Heather Lynn.

For twenty-six years, John served as a principal with six different public schools in S. D. and G. He ended his education career in 1999.

This was a banner year in John's life. He married, bought a new home, retired and started a new career as a life insurance agent and financial advisor with CLARICA (later to become Sun Life Financial), the latter career lasted for the next ten years.

He has been active in his community serving in many volunteer capacities with the Canadian Cancer Society, the Cornwall Community Hospital Foundation, Knox-St. Paul's United Church, Meals-on-Wheels, and the Cornwall Curling Club.

He enjoys gardening, biking, walking, entertaining, vacations on Anna Maria Island in Florida, curling and most importantly spending time with his children, grandchildren, step grandchildren, and step great grandchild.

On June 8, 1973, John married Mary Heather (Dewar) Harland at Cornwall's Knox United Church. They had James Andrew McMaster Irvine and Jonathan Edward Marshall Irvine. In 1989 Mary and John divorced, John receiving full custody of James and Jonathan.

James Andrew McMaster Irvine (1978) married Sonya Joyce Lockyer (1979) in 2012 and they have Olivia Molly Irvine (2012) and Parker Peter James Irvine (2016).

Jonathan Edward Marshall Irvine (1980), has partner Tarah Zaczyk (1983) who has Olive Harrop (2009) and Indie Harrop (2011).

Mary had Heather Lynn Harland (1965) by a previous marriage. Lynn married James Maxim Maingot October 17, 1987 and they had Madelyne Mary Maingot (1990). Lynn and James divorced in 1999.

John Marshall Irvine married (2nd) Gloria Elizabeth (Napp) McFaul (1951) in 1999.

Gloria had three children from her previous marriage to John Edmund McFaul; Shannon Darcy McFaul (1974), Cynthia Leigh McFaul (1977) and Blake Johnathon McFaul (1983).

Shannon married Michael David LaBier (1969) on June 26th, 2007 and has Jessica Elizabeth Drew Watters-McFaul (1992). Jessica has Keira Leigh Farrel (2012).

Cynthia never married but has Adrianne Leigh Keeler-McFaul (2007).

Blake married Claire Christine Gibbs (1983) and has Malcolm Blake McFaul (2015).

Douglas Marshall Irvine (1952) *(John, John, John Edward, Arthur Marshall, Arthur Marshall)*

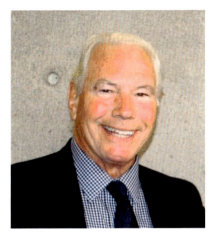

Douglas Marshall Irvine

Douglas Marshall Irvine was born May 31, 1952 at the Cornwall General Hospital, but returned home to find his parents Margaret Mona McMaster and Arthur Marshall Irvine busy wondering how they had managed to have a child so late in life.

Early childhood memories were filled with great travel, Central Public Elementary, lacrosse, Camp On-da-da-wa on Golden Lake, and most of all, discovering the freedom that comes with a summer cottage; carefree days spent boating and swimming on the St. Lawrence. (at Stonehouse Point and later Hamilton's Island, both a short drive from Cornwall).

Doug turned ten and Marsh was transferred to a new Domtar research centre in Senneville, PQ and the family of four ventured into the West Island of Montreal to a town on Lac St. Louis called Baie d'urfe where Doug would spend his formative years (10-16) learning about hockey, baseball, skiing, sailing, music, skateboarding and academic life at MacDonald High School in Ste. Anne de Bellevue.

By his final year in the Baie, (1967) brother David and his wife Sylvia purchased the Harbour View summer resort in Smith's Cove, Digby County, Nova Scotia and Doug was given his first summer job. Working as a painter, mower, lifeguard, bicycle renter, desk clerk, and snack shop operator, several summers were spent enjoying the sun, fun and life-long friendships of the resort.

After four years at St. Patrick's College and Carleton University in Ottawa, he graduated with an honours BA in English Literature, forged on to Acadia University in Wolfville where he graduated with a Bachelor of Education ('77). For eight months spanning 1974-'75, the year was spent traveling throughout Europe after working at a train station restaurant in Zug, Switzerland. Doug took a leave of absence in 1989 from Hantsport School to complete his Masters in Education from Acadia working part-time in their library.

As teachers, Nancy and Doug were afforded wonderful summers at their cottage called "Duck Downs"; an hour and a half drive from their adopted hometown of Hantsport on the Avon River. The cottage was resurrected on a lot purchased from the resort where the "Hidden Hearth" summer home had burned in 1962. Time in Smith's Cove was spent with plenty of family and friends enjoying beach parties, boating trips to Bear Island, sailboat races in the Annapolis Basin, camping trips to Kejimkujik National Park, and endless hours swimming at the Harbour View pool.

Doug retired from a lifelong one-school career as Junior High Language Arts and Social Studies teacher at Hantsport School in 2011. He continued his love of teaching as a substitute for the next five years until Nancy sought full-time retirement and they concentrated on completing their cottage in the Cove.

These days Doug participates in community efforts as a board member of the Smith's Cove Historical Society and the Sulis-Smith Cemetery Committee. Doug also spent two two-year terms as President of the

Harbourview Cottagers' Association. Recent honours include his induction into the Military and Hospitaller Order of St. Lazurus (2017).

Douglas Marshall Irvine married Nancy Ruth Prescesky (1958) of Montreal in the Birch Chapel at Harbour View in 1980 and they had Dylan McMaster Irvine (1984) and Nataleah Rae Irvine (1990).
Dylan married Meaghan Lindsay Bunton (1984) in 2010 and they have Jack William McMaster Irvine (2016).
Nataleah's partner is Gregory Alan Hanlon (1989)

Wendy Jane Irvine (1940) *(John, John, John Edward, Arthur Marshall, Lawrence Craibe)*

Wendy married Arthur George Plumb (1919-2006). They had Jane Elizabeth Plumb (1968), who married (1st) Lindsay Neil Perlman, since divorced. They had Hannah Meryl Pearlman (1994) and Jonah Michael Pearlman (1997). Jane married (2nd) Rodney Yale Kaufman (1967). Wendy lives in Toronto, a few blocks awat from Jane and her family.

Linda Carole Irvine (1944) *(John, John, John Edward, Arthur Marshall, Lawrence Craibe)*

Carole married (1st) Clifford Kurz, since divorced, followed by her marriage (2nd) to fellow musician, Manfred Eberhardt Liebert (1934) in Woelfersheim, Germany.

Robert Lawrence Irvine (1947-2001) *(John, John, John Edward, Arthur Marshall, Lawrence Craibe)*

Jaqueline (Jaci) Godman Irvine (1948) *(John, John, John Edward, William Henry, Henry Erskine Bryant Irvine)*

Jaci Godman Irvine, is divorced from her first husband Richard Harwell, and has two children by her second husband Michael Harman, from whom she is also divorced. They had Tamarind Valborg Harman (1982), who lives in Carpinteria, CA and Thorin Bryant Harman (1984), who lives in Howell, MI. She married Nicholas J. Hopes (1964) of London, UK in 2015. They live at present in Folkestone, UK.

Carola Godman Irvine (1951) *(John, John, John Edward, William Henry, Henry Erskine Bryant Irvine*

Carola Godman Irvine is divorced from Victor Richard Law, an international banker (1941) of Edinburgh, Scotland, who she married 10 June 1982 in the Guard's Chapel in London. Victor was serving in the Guards at the time. They had three children: Mathew Frederic Harry Godman Law (1983), who lives in Singapore, Charley Victor Colton Law (1984) and Catrina (Nina) Clare Law (1987), who live at home. All three children were born in London.

Bonnie M. Irvine (1936) *(John, John, Hugh Marshall, John Alfred, Hugh Avery)*

Noel Barrie Irvine (1937) *(John, John, Hugh Marshall, John Alfred, Hugh Avery)*

> Noel's children: Derek William Barry Irvine (1971) and Graham Stuart Hugh Irvine (1972)

> Graham's child: Logan Robert Irvine (2008)

Tanga Delance Rose Irvine (1946) *(John, John, Hugh Marshall, John Alfred, Hugh Avery)*

Victoria Stan-lee Irvine (1950) *(John, John, Hugh Marshall, John Alfred, Hugh Avery)*

Carol Denise Irvine (1939) *(John, John, Hugh Marshall, John Alfred, William Douglas)*

Raymond Douglas Irvine (1950) *(John, John, Hugh Marshall, John Alfred, William Douglas)*

> Raymond's children: Jessica Rae Irvine (1974) and Matthew Alan Irvine (1979)

Wayne John Irvine (1958) *(John, John, Hugh Marshall, John Alfred, John Alexander)*

Harland Stewart Irvine (1952-2017) *(John, John, Hugh Marshall, John Alfred, Wilfrerd Harland)*

> Harland Stewart's children: Sarah Jane Irvine (1970), Bronwyn Elizabeth Irvine (1981) and Brody John Irvine (1985)

David John Irvine (1956) *(John, John, Hugh Marshall, John Alfred, Wilfrerd Harland)*

> David John's children: Melissa Ann Irvine (1980), Hayley Joy Irvine (1993) and Chandra Marie Irvine (1996)

APPENDICES

1. The Border Reivers – Including the Irvines

For over 350 years up to the end of the 16th century, what are now Northumberland, Cumbria, The Scottish Borders, Dumfries, and Galloway rang to the clash of steel and thunder of hooves. As George MacDonald Fraser explains in his book, <u>The Steel Bonnets</u>,

> The great border tribes of both Scotland and England feuded continuously among themselves. Robbery and blackmail were everyday professions; raiding, arson, kidnapping, murder, and extortion were an accepted part of the social system. While the monarchs of England and Scotland ruled the comparatively secure hearts of their kingdoms, the narrow hill land between was dominated by the lance and the sword. The tribal leaders from their towers, the broken men, and outlaws of the mosses, the ordinary peasants of the valleys, in their own phrase, 'shook loose the Border'. They continued to shake it as long as it was political reality, practising systematic robbery and destruction on each other. History has christened them the Border Reivers.
>
> In the story of Britain, the Border Reiver is a unique figure. He was not part of a separate minority group in his area; he came from every social class. He was an agricultural labourer, or a small-holder, or a gentleman farmer, or even a peer of the realm, a professional cattle rustler, a fighting man and a guerrilla soldier of great resource to whom the arts of theft, raid, tracking, and ambush were second nature. He was also a gangster organized on highly professional lines, who had perfected the protection racket three centuries before Chicago was built. He gave blackmail to the English language.

Throughout the Reiving years, travel was dangerous business. Strangers met with suspicion, fear and hostility. The traveller had to move cautiously by day, always sought shelter before nightfall and rarely found a welcome.

The Border Lands, territorial patch of the Border Reiver, straddle the once disputed boundary and Debatable Land between "two of the most energetic, aggressive, talented and all together formidable nations in history", England and Scotland. They stretch in one broad sweep from the Solway Firth in the west to the Northumbrian and Berwickshire coast in the east and comprise the Cheviot Hills and parts of the Southern Uplands and the Pennines. To the west, they are the Solway Coast and the Eden Valley, to the east, the Merse. They are riven by the waters of the Nith, the Annan, the Esk, the Teviot, the Tweed, and by Redesdale, Coquetdale, Tynedale and, of course Liddesdale, scene of so many of the bloodiest events of the Reiving years.

The Border lands are home to the descendants of the notorious Reivers and their marauding families: the Armstrongs, the Grahams, the Irvines, the Kerrs, the Scotts, the Elliots, the Maxwells, the Johnstones, the Musgraves, the Bells, the Fosters, the Charltons, the Nixons and the Robsons to name just some of the more feuding elements of Border society in the 16th century. The area is liberally dotted with castles, stately homes, the ruins of historic abbeys, fortified farmhouses (bastles), the scattered remains of pele towers and the atmospheric remnants of abandoned hamlets or howfs, hidden up remote side valleys. The many towns and settlements that were raided, the fortified churches and the defensive walls and dykes dating back to Elizabeth I and her forbears. The fields of battle and the Reiver graveyards all bear testament to the turbulent history that marked these lands and those times. The brutal activities of the warring families and the indiscriminate plundering and merciless cruelty that drove fear deep into the very souls of ordinary Border folk.

Other vestiges of that virtually ungovernable region, of that lawless state that was allowed to flourish, more or less unchecked, for the best part of 350 years, reside within the ancient seats of power, the Warden families such as the Buccleuchs, Dacres, Humes and Scropes, the frontier garrisons, the places of truce. And on the Reiver side, there are the secret places of sanctuary, the lairs they fled to in the heat of pursuit, the 'hot trod'; mosses and wastes where pursuing posses could find themselves at a distinct disadvantage; hidden valleys where one thousand head of cattle could be spirited away.

2. History of The Irvines

No attempt will be made here to cover the history of the Irvines. To do so would require a large book. But there are some interesting facts about the Irvines, which should be included in any genealogy.

The Irvines are one of the oldest clans in Scotland. They are also one of the widest dispersed Scottish families around the world. In 1004 A.D. Crinun Erevin (an old spelling of Irvine) "Abtnane of Dule" married Beatrix daughter of Malcomn II King of Scotland. Their son Duncan I became King of Scotland in 1034 A.D. From 1034 A.D. to the reign of John Baliol all the Rulers of Scotland were descended from Crinun Erevin. Which simply means all the kings of Scotland from Duncan I (1034 A.D.) to John Baliol were descended from the male Irvine line. The exception was McBeth who ruled from 1040 A.D. to 1057 A.D. He was slain by Malcolm III, who was dethroned by his son Duncan II, who was dispossessed by Edgar son of Malcolm III. He was succeeded by Alexander I called "The Fierce" in 1107 A.D. Each of these was an Irvine descendent. Robert de Bruce was descended in the female line from David Erevine, Earl of Huntington, a brother of Malcolm IV and William King of Scots.

The Irvine male line appears to have ruled Scotland from 1034 A.D. to the death of Alexander III in 1285 A.D. And with two exceptions of seventy years, in the female line until 1678. (This is from the book The Irvines and Their Kin).

The Irvines along with the Johnstons and other clans were nearly wiped out by the English during the wars of suppression. It was during this period that many Scots fled to Ireland. We do not know when the Irvines settled in Ireland, but it seems logical that it was during this period that they left Scotland.

The Irvines were fighters. As far back as the 10th century one of the strongest Scottish clans were the Irvines. They built towers (castles) along the border with England to protect themselves. These towers withstood many attacks by the British. The Irvine tower of Bonshaw was raided and burned many times, but withstood the attacks and stands today. It is still the seat of the Bonshaw Irvine clan.

Many of the Scots who left Scotland and settled in Ireland found their troubles were not over. They had continuing religious problems and suffered suppression by land owners. During this period, many Scotch-Irish left Scotland for America.

Anyone interested in the history of the Irvines should attempt to obtain one or more of these books:

The Irvines and Their Kin. Compiled by L. Boyd. This summarizes the history of the Irvines in Scotland. It covers the period from 373 A.D. to 1906. Unfortunately, it is out of print but a copy of it was left to Helen Irvine by her father John Quincey Adams Irvine.

The Book of the Irvings, Irvins, Irvines, or Erinevines. By John Beaufin Irvin, Chieftain of Bonshaw in Scotland. (Also out of print) Both of the above books are available in the library of Congress. The regional genealogical offices of the Church of the Latter-Day Saints, have these books in micro-film.

The Irvines of Bonshaw. By Alastair M.T. Maxwell Irvine, of the house of "Irving of Dumfries". It was written in 1968 reprinted in 1983. Available from Bonshaw Tower, Kertlebridge, Lockerbie Dumfrieshire, Scotland, DG ll-3LY.

Erwins and Related Families. By Frances Erwin Evans, a history of migration of the Irvines/Erwins through Scotland and Ireland, this provides a history of many who came to Philadelphia and then moved south through Bucks and Chester Counties, Pennsylvania and then to the Carolinas and Georgia. This book is available from Mrs. Francis Erwin Evans, 967 Foster's Mill Road S.W. Rome, GA 30161.

3. The Irvines Of Castle Irvine

Pynnar, in his Special Census of Northern Ireland in 1618-1619, reported that Gerard Lowther had built a house and a strong bawn made of lime and stone. The bawn was 324 feet in circumference and the walls were 17 feet high. Near the bawn was a village consisting of 10 houses, a market house, and a water mill. At first this was called Lowtherstown, but later changed its name to Irvinestown.

Gerard Lowther died in 1629 and his godson, also called Gerard, inherited the property. He was married three times but had no children. He leased the land to Christopher Irvine who was related to him by marriage.

The author in front of Castle Irvine, Irvinestown, Ireland

The Irish rebellion of 1641 was felt locally. Christopher Irvine and his family were forced to flee to Enniskillen Castle for safety. Castle Irvine was burnt down in their absence. The Irvines were Royalists and supporters of Charles I and his men. In the Williamite wars they were to be found on the side of James II. However, by the end of the wars the family appeared to have a change of heart and Gerard Irvine died in William III's service. The Irvines like the Lowthers were of Scottish origin, related to the Irvings of Bonshaw, Dumfriesshire. They quickly settled in County Fermanagh and, married into their local planter families. In 1788, Major George Marcus Irvine married Elizabeth, daughter and heiress of Judge D'Arcy of Dunmow Castle, County Meath. It was at that time that D'Arcy was added to the Irvine family name.

The castle that we see today is of the 19th century period, since Judge D'Arcy had renovations carried out in 1831. The original 17th century round towers were kept at the back of the castle and the front was extended to make a two-story range built in Tudor Gothic style with octagonal turrets at the corners. The gate lodge on the Enniskillen road reflects in miniature the mixtures of styles at the castle. The Irvines were in residence until 1922 when Major D'Arcy Irvine decided to leave for England. With him went the last remaining family connections with the castle and town. The castle is now known as Necarne Castle and was boarded up and deserted when Sylvia and I visited it a few years ago. The grounds and some of the barns and out-buildings support the Ulster Lakeland Equestrian Park.

(The book Necarne Castle and the Ulster Lakeland Equestrian Park, Breege McCusker, 1995, pg. 3-4 may be purchased directly from the author for £3.50. Breege McCusker, Drumharvey, Irvinestown, Co. Fermanagh, N. Ireland, BT94)

4. Various Irvine Crests

Irvings of Bonshaw
HAUD ULLIS
LABENTIA VENTIS

*YIELDING UNDER
NO WINDS*

Irvines of Drum
SUB SOLE
SUB UMBRA VIRENS

*FLOURISHING IN SUN
AND SHADE*

5. Ships Built by Hugh Irvine and Brothers in Saint John

EDINA, July 1839, 471-ton barque

RAMAY, December 1839, 680-ton ship

HANNAH KERR, 1840, 695-ton ship

GLENLYON, August 1841, 909-ton ship

ARGIMOU, July 1844, 176-ton barque (Built by Hugh alone)

VIXEN, November 1845, 175-ton brigantine

ELF, 1846, 129-ton brigantine

HARBINGER, 1847, 113-ton schooner

CRANSTON, 1847, 809-ton ship

STAR, 1848, 728-ton ship

SAINT JOHN, 1847, steamer

EL DORADO, 1848, 842-ton ship

MAHTOREE, 1848, 306-ton barque

IOWA, 1849, 880-ton ship (John was on this ship when he died of cholera in Quebec City)

OTTILLIA, 1850, 923-ton ship (the last built by Hugh)

6. Four Letters from John Irvine to Lovicia - 1849

Liverpool, July 7th, 1849

Dear Wife:

It is with pleasure I sit down to send you a few lines to let you know that I am well. Hoping this will find you all enjoying the same blessings. I received your letter yesterday, and I was glad to hear you were all well. We had a long passage, the wind being light and from the eastward, pretty much all the passage. I will not have much time to write you all the particulars this mail, as I am on board of the ship in this stream, and I have only got an hour from this to get it to the post office before the mails close.

We arrived yesterday and had to go ashore and to see about getting the ship docked today, so you will have to excuse me if I do not give you more particulars by this mail, but I hope by next to give you full particulars.

You will give my love to Hannah and to John, Howard and his wife, and Margaret, and all the rest of our friends. Give my respect to Thomas Irvine, and tell him I am well. I hope you will make yourself happy until I return, which I hope, will not be very long if I am spared in health. Give my love to the children and tell Alexander that I hope he will be a good boy and mind what you say to him. Give my respects to all inquiring friends, So no more present but remain your affectionate and loving husband, until death do us part.

John Irvine

Liverpool, July 28th, 1849

Dear Wife:

I take this opportunity of sending you a few lines to let you know that I am well. Hoping this will find you all enjoying the same blessings, which we ought to be thankful to God for.

I have not much news to write you. We only got the ship discharged last night. I an in hopes she will be sold by next mail, so that I may get home again to see you, but although we are apart I trust that our prayers are united at the throne of Grace, from which I hope, all our comforts proceed.

Give my love to Hannah, John Stewart, and Grace, Margaret and all inquiring friends. Thomas Irvine arrived last evening. He is well and wishes to be remembered to you all. He says you will be fretting about me. I hope you will make yourself contented till I return, as we still have the same

protector wherever we are.

I hope Alexander and the children will be good boys till I return. My time is short this morning as I was along with Thomas to the office, and it closes at 12:00 o'clock.

No more, but remain your affectionate and loving husband until death do us part.

John Irvine

Liverpool August 18th, 1849

Dear Wife

It is with pleasure that I send you a few lines to let you know that I am well hoping this will find you all enjoying the same blessings.. I expected to have left this mail but as the ship is not sold I think I shall come out in her to Quebeck to save expense. She may sell yet before we go as there is parties after her which I trust she may as I feel anxious to get home. I hope you will make your mind contented till I arrive as we have still the same protector wherever we are in this world and I hope our prayers is enacted at the throne of Grace from which all our consolation do proceed.

You will give my love to Hannah and to John Stewart and Grace and all our friends. I have kept back writing to the last minute so that I have not time to write you a long letter. I shall write to you for to go by next mail if the ship is sold I will be out by her myself. Thomas Irvine is coming to St. John's. They send their kind love to you. Give my best love to all our friends and tell them I am well and in hopes to see you soon. I remain your affectionate and loving Husband until death do us part.

John Irvine

Quebeck October 5th, 1849

Dear Wife

I take this opportunity of sending you a few lines to let you know that I am well hoping this will find you all enjoying the same blessing.

We had a pretty long passage out. We were 17 days after we made the land before we got up to Quebeck. We had a pilot aboard 12 days. We arrived on Tuesday last but there was no mail till today for St. Johns. I expected there might have been a letter from you on my arrival but I was disappointed. When you receive this you will write as soon as possible and let me know how you all are. I cannot tell you exactly what time I will be able to leave this for St. John but I think it will be about three weeks.

If all goes well I shall write to you every week. I have not got anything particular to write only hoping you have not fretted about me being away so long for we have the same protector on the Sea as on the land. You will give my love to Hannah and tell her that I hope she has kept your spirits up while I have been gone. Give my regards to John and Grace and Margaret and to all our friends. I hope the children has been good boys while I have been gone. So no more at present. But in hopes to see you soon.

I remain your affectionate and Loving Husband

John Irvine

7. St. Andrew's Society Medals

8. Tribute to John E Irvine

John Edward Irvine (1846-1911) was listed as a Member of the Saint John St. Andrew's Society in 1890, and was a Member until he moved to Calgary in 1905. The following appeared in the Saint John newspaper in 1905 entitled: "Another Resolution for John E. Irvine".

> The Saint Andrew's Society have presented John E. Irvine, one of their Members with the following address:
>
> Dear Sir and Brother: The Saint Andrew's Society of the city of Saint John learns with deep regret you are about to remove from our midst and seek a new home in our great Northwest. For some 16 years you have been an honoured member of our Society and have largely contributed to the pleasure and entertainment of our meetings, and we cannot part from you without expressing our deep regret at separation.
>
> We desire to bear testimony to your worth as a public-spirited citizen, largely interested in organizing and conducting many of the charitable and Christian institutions in our city. Your departure from our midst will be felt as a public loss, and we trust you may in your new field of labour find ample scope to exercise your charitable and philanthropic desires.
>
> In parting from you we wish you every success and warmly commend you to the fraternal regard of all true and faithful Scots wherever you may be.

9. Page from the White Family History Re: Julia Elvira (White) Irvine

William Henry White, third son of Vincent and Mary (Dykeman) White, was born at Grand Lake, Queens County, New Brunswick, August 12, 1820; he married (1) Sarah Miers, February 28, 1844; she died June 21, 1848, aged twenty-three years; no issue; married (2) Eliza Jane Hatfield, March 10, 1852 who died in August 1886, leaving five children; married (3) Emily M. Mott, September 24, 1889; no issue; he died February 19, 1901.

William H. White

William H. White began his business career in partnership with his brother James E. They first opened a general store at White's Corner, Springfieled, Kings County, and about three years later established a branch store at Belleisle Point. Their brothers Gilbert and Samual, who had carried on storekeeping at Grand Lake, closed up their Queens County businesses and shortly after William H. and James E. had opened the store at Belleisle Point, came into the business as partners and the firm name being thereupon changed from W. H. & J. E. White to White & Brothers. This partnership, after some four or five years, was disolved, and thereafter William H. and James E. continued the business together, save for a brief time, during which Gilbert and Samuel returned to the firm. About 1851 the brothers William H. and James E. opened a branch store at Sussex and James E. moved to Sussex to take charge of the business. Later their brother Hiram was taken into the business, and later still their brother Charles T. became a partner. The firm name was changed to White Bros., and a wholesale general store was opened by this firm in Saint John, relating to which the old stores at White's Corner and Sussex were continued as branches, and additional branches were established at Apohaqui and Smith's Creek, Kings County. The firm of White Bros. for years did a large and thriving business. William H. and James E. retired from the firm in the early seventies, William H. going to Sussex to live while James E. continued to live in St. John.

Children by second wife:

95. I. – **Julia, Elvira, born January 8, 1852; issue, five.**
96. II. – Marianna, born July 10, 1855; issue three.
97. III. – Daniel Wesley Hatfield, born February 16, 1860; issue, four.
98. IV. – Laura Eliza, born March 8, 1867; issue, three.
  V. – Lillian Alice, born August 16, 1874; unmarried.

10. Closing the Estate of Hugh Marshall Irvine

Annapolis Spectator, Friday, March 9, 1894:

FOR SALE Real Estate, Shipping STOCK & c.

To close Estate of Troop & Irvine

The Assignees offer the following property for sale. If not sold on or before the 22d day of March next will be sold at PUBLIC AUCTION on said day at 2 o'clock at Granville Ferry.

1. The undivided half part of that parcel of land in Granville Ferry and known as the Tenement House property situated on the back Street.
2. House, land and premises at Granville Ferry at present occupied by H.M. Irvine.
3. All that parcel of land in Granville Ferry known as the Hotel property formerly owned by Alfred L. Troop and James H. Rhodes.
4. House and farm premises at Granville Ferry occupied by A.L. Troop bounded on the west by Wm. Meikel, Israel Letteney, SWW Pickup, Wm. Brothers; Estate and Robert Delap's land, Northerly by land of Stephen Hall; Easterly by lands of Charles Troop, Alexander Irvin and the Troop barn; Also that piece of marsh land being part of Mount Ann marsh, bounded by Parker Creek; Easterly by Stephen Troop, Southerly by marsh belonging to Israel Troop; and west by marsh belonging to James M. Gilliatt. Also another piece of marsh land being part of Mount Ann marsh in the Township of Granville, containing 2 ¾ acres.
5. That parcel of land and premises at Granville Ferry, bounded on the north by Robert Delap; Easterly by lands belonging to Estate of Samuel McCormick, and Westerly by Walter Willett, and Southerly by Water Street; together with store, warehouse, etc.
6. That piece of woodland on the North Mountain bounded on the east and south by lands of Israel Trask; Westerly by lands of John Oliver.
7. The undivided half part of that wharf property known as the Letteney Wharf.
8. That other parcel of land in the Township of Granville being part of Farm Lot #40, beginning at the public highway bounded on the north by lands of Israel Letteney; east by James Hall; west by lands belonging to Israel Letteny and south by the main road.
SHIPPING STOCK, etc
5 shares Fundy SS Co.
5 shares Acadia SS Co.
4-64 shares brigt Nellie Pickup
2-64 shares sch Lena Pickup
1-64 shares sch Bartholdl 2
4-64 shares sch Granville
2-64 shares bark James Stafford
10 Shares Valley Telephone Co.
6 2-year old Heifers
1 3-year old Colt
All accounts and notes of hand not settled at once will be left for collection.
John E. Irvine SWW Pickup, Assignee

11. *The Beaver* Magazine Article on AMI

Close of French Government Transport Work

A. M. Irvine and Staff Leave Service With Shutting of Montreal Agency; Great War Work of H.B.C. Recalled

AS the work of H.B.C. in connection with transportation matters for the French government was terminated March 31st, a number of necessary changes have been made in the Company's Montreal organization.

Mr. A. M. Irvine, general agent, and several of his staff have resigned from the service.

The inception of the H.B.C. Montreal agency was occasioned by the extensive purchasing and transport work which the Company took in hand for the French government during the fall of 1914.

The Company was appointed the purchasing agent in North America for goods required by the French military establishment. Later this arrangement was extended so that H.B.C. was entrusted with the purchase and transport of grain, flour and other food-stuffs which the French government provided for civilian needs.

During the five years, 1915 to 1919, the quantity of goods transported in H.B.C. ships exceeded 13,000,000 tons.

The Company purchased and financed on behalf of the French government a fleet of approximately 225,000 tons, deadweight, for carrying these supplies. Although more than two-fifths of this tonnage was sunk by enemy submarines, no less than 350 voyages were made by these steamers, covering a total mileage of over 2,500,000. In addition, a large number of vessels were time-chartered, so that at one period during the war the total tonnage of ships under H.B.C. management exceeded 1,000,000. At the end of December, 1919, there was a total of 286 vessels loading under the Company's organization.

In addition to the Montreal agency, under the charge of Mr. A. M. Irvine, there was created a network of H.B.C. agencies, numbering 145, at the ports of discharge in France and other shipping centres throughout the world.

The closing of the H.B.C. Montreal agency at the termination of the French government contracts marks an epoch in the Company's history, during which it was privileged to render great service in the world war and at the outset of reconstruction.

12. Hudson Bay Company Cap Badge and Medal

13. James H. and Margaret Elizabeth (Robinson) Roop Gravestones, Roop Family Cemetery

14. Article from Cornwall Paper, September 2, 1941

CORNWALL, ONTARIO, TUESDAY, SEPTEMBER 2, 1941

Canada's Third Division Is Ranked
Among Best Of Dominion's Forces

LT. A. M. IRVINE

Eastern Ontario Regiment "Feels At Home" Going Through Bren Gun Drill Under Cornwall Officer

By DOUGLAS AMARON
Canadian Press Staff Writer

SOMEWHERE IN ENGLAND, Sept. 2—(CP)—Canadian soldiers of the 3rd Division, latest reinforcements for the Dominion's overseas army, are adjusting themselves quickly to their new life in Great Britain.

Ranked among the fittest and best-trained men to come from Canada, these soldiers spent the first month since their arrival polishing up on route marches, bayonet practice, rifle drill and other first [...] of soldiering.

Pte. A. Allaston   Pte. D. McCoshen

Pte. R. Leathem   Sgt. P. Sporring

15. Memorabilia – The War Years

PRINCIPLES OF WAR
CWSC 7
July 43

1. Concentration - superior force decisive time & place.
2. Economy force -
3. Surprise - speed. deception
4. Mobility - staff work - physical fitness - mech fitness.
5. Offensive action
6. Cooperation - liaison
7. Security
8. Maintenance of object - determination.

BASIC PTS

1. Stage management of battle - staff work
2. Battle drills for all procedure. HQ, recce et
3. Individual - and sub unit efficiency
4. Morale, fighting spirit, discipline.

1. Initial soundness of disposns & forms
2. Staff arrangements - keep flexible.
3. Good comms.

Fight only when superior in all ways.

Consider - Nature, time, ground, air, comms
sup, morale, relative str.

Marsh's notes, #7 Canadian War Staff Course, Royal Military College

From Brigadier A E Walford

Tac HQ First Cdn Army
Cdn Army England

29 Apr 44

Dear Marsh —

I received a letter today from Brig Roberts
which I have shown to the Army Comd. The following is
an extract:

"I want to tell you how very grateful I am to
you for having loaned Baldwin and Irvine to
this Headquarters to help us with our planning.
It was extremely kind of you to give us this
assistance and I can assure you that it was
very greatly appreciated. Baldwin and Irvine have
both done very well indeed and I only hope that
they have been able to gain some benefit from
their attachment here. They strike me as being
very efficient staff officers and we were all
very sorry when they left."

I am very pleased to know that you and Baldwin
created such a good impression at Second Army HQ and were
of assistance to them. The Army Comd has seen
cheery msl

Sincerely,
A E Walford

Capt A M Irvine
Cdn Sec HUCO West
21 Army Gp
No 1 ADPC

Letter of commendation

109

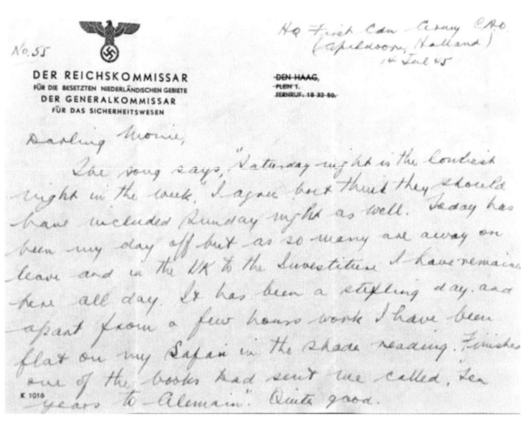

No. 55

DER REICHSKOMMISSAR
FÜR DIE BESETZTEN NIEDERLÄNDISCHEN GEBIETE
DER GENERALKOMMISSAR
FÜR DAS SICHERHEITSWESEN

DEN HAAG,
PLEIN 1.
FERNRUF. 18-32-50.

HQ First Cdn. Army C.A.D.
(Apeldoorn, Holland)
14 Jul 45

Darling Monie,

The song says, "Saturday night is the loneliest night in the week." I agree but think they should have included Sunday night as well. Today has been my day off but as so many are away on leave and in the UK to the Investiture I have remained here all day. It has been a stifling day and apart from a few hours work I have been flat on my Safari in the shade reading. Finished one of the books had sent me called "Ten years to Alamein." Quite good.

K 1016

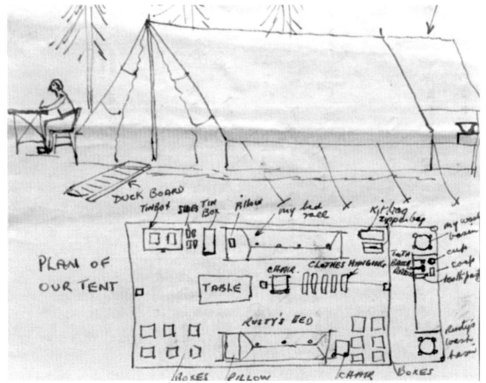

A letter home to daughter Mona Lou on July 14, 1945 explaining their tent set-up on captured German letterhead

FIRST CDN ARMY

STAFF AND SERVICE OFFICERS

REALLOCATION QUESTIONNAIRE

1. Rank... _MAJOR (Confirmed)_
   (Indicate whether acting or confirmed)

2. SURNAME (in block letters)... _IRVINE_

3. CHRISTIAN NAMES (in full). _ARTHUR MARSHALL_

4. Married.. _Yes_ ....Single........Widower.......

   Widower or divorcee with dependent children.......

   Children and ages. _three - aged 12, 10, 1 yr._

5. DATE OF BIRTH... _15_   _MAR_   _1906_
                    (day)   (month)   (year)

6. JOINED ARMY.. _21 JUN 1940 (AF)... 8 Sep 1938 (NPAM)_

7. SERVICE. _Pk Comd 1940-42, A2nt-Jun-Aug 1942_
   SLQ' 1 Can Corps Sep-Nov 42, SCQ 1 Can Corps DEC-APR '43
   7CWSC MAY-Nov 43 SCQ Can Planning Staff Dec-43-
   MAR 44, GSO2(2) APR 44 - date.

8. DECORATIONS...
   CVSM & MID. Nil

9. MEDICAL CATEGORY... _A_ .... or grading _06 1111111_
                              YOR PULHEMS

10. PRESENT APPOINTMENT.. _GSO 2 LIAISON ADM_

11. POINTS (add 20% if married).... _184_

12. FAR EAST FORCE   YES_____ NO _X_
                          (insert X in applicable space)

13. OCCUPATIONAL FORCE YES_____ NO _X_
                          (insert X in applicable space)

14. RETURN TO CANADA   YES _X_   NO_____
                          (insert X in applicable space)

    (If it is desired to indicate priority place numerals
    1, 2, etc, after 'X')

                              Signature... _Art Irvine_
                                            Maj

To be completed and returned in duplicate through normal
channels to:

        Dep Mil Sec
        Main HQ First Cdn Army

Application for repatriation home

111

11th August 1946 - <u>Exact Wording of Citation</u>

Award of "Member of the Most Excellent Order of the British Empire"
to Major Arthur Marshall Irvine 31st January 1945.

        It has been due in large measure to this officer's drive
and enthusiasm that the Administrative Liaison Section at Headquarters
First Canadian Army has come to play an increasingly important part
in the Administration of First Canadian Army.

        In recent months in particular the work and leadership of
this outstanding Officer have contributed in no small measure to
the successful administration of First Canadian Army.   This covered
the period from Rouen, France, through Belgium, including the
capture of Le Havre, Calais, Ghent, Antwerp, Bruges, the Scheldt
Estuary, and into Holland as far as Nimegan.

        The Dutch decoration or Order covered the period from
31st January 1945 to the end of the war in May 1945.

Member of the Order of British Empire citation

<u>Later.</u> Sun 20 Aug 44

Have just arrived back at HQ after a very interesting trip by Jeep of 160 miles today most of it through country which has been fought over during the past week or so. Sorry I cannot tell you more about it.

Fraser Gill arrived to join us while I was away. Very glad to see him.

Jack Clarry and Schmidlin from our course arrived on this side today. Both were at Knee as DS.

Found piles of mail awaiting me and as soon as I have read it all will try to drop you another line.

All my love darling.
Kiss the three rascals for me.
Always your
Marsh.

Letter home, 1944

113

16. Stonehouse Point Historic Site

Glengarry House National Historic Site of Canada is located on Stonehouse Point, just east of Cornwall, Ontario. Now a ruin, the fieldstone gable walls of the house are overgrown by thick brush. The house was likely built in 1792 by Lieutenant Colonel John Macdonell, the first Speaker of the Legislative Assembly of Upper Canada and a pioneer in the settlement of Ontario.

Glengarry House was designated a national historic site of Canada in 1921.

John Macdonell received a land grant from the Crown at the conclusion of the American Revolution in recognition of his military service. Although he likely first constructed a log dwelling, it was recorded that he had almost completed a large fieldstone house near the

shore of the St. Lawrence River in 1792. Macdonell called the house Glengarry House. It is unclear what happened to the house after Macdonell's death. During the War of 1812, it was converted into a barracks for the local militia and was badly damaged by the soldiers. There is a local tradition that the house burned in 1813, but this seems unlikely, since claims were made in 1815 and 1825 to the British authorities for the cost of repairs. By the 1890s, the building was in ruin with only the gable walls standing.

Former Commander Of S D and Gs Arthur Irvine Dies At Age 64

A well-known and respected Cornwall resident and a former lieutenant colonel of the SD and G Highlanders, died yesterday in Cornwall General Hospital at the age of 64.

Arthur Marshall Irvine, formerly of 512 James St., is resting at McArthur Bros. and MacNeil Funeral Home where friends may call today and Sunday.

A private funeral service will be conducted Monday, by Rev. Claire Kellogg followed by commital services and cremation at 2 p.m. in Mount Royal Cemetery, Montreal.

Mr. Irvine, born in St. John, N.B., was the son of the late Arthur and Lulah Marshall.

He received his post-high school education at Ashbury College in Ottawa and McGill University, Montreal.

Mr. Irvine was an employee of Howard Smith Paper Mills Ltd. here from 1933 to 1963. He then moved to Baie D'urfe, Que., where he was administrator of the Domtar research plant, at Senneville, until he retired in 1969.

His military career describes the type of man he was.

He first enlisted in the SD and G Highlanders Reserve in 1938 and went into active duty with the Regiment on Aug. 26, 1939.

In June 1940 he joined the First Battalion overseas as second lieutenant, later he was transferred to adjutant of the First Canadian Corps Headquarters with the rank of captain.

He returned to Canada in 1943 to attend Canadian War Staff College at the Royal Military College, Kingston, returning to London that Fall as staff cap-

ARTHUR IRVINE

tain of the Canadian Planning Staff.

Mr. Irvine was promoted to major when he was posted to the First Canadian Army Headquarters and subsequently seconded to the second British Army Headquarters.

Just prior to the invasion of France he returned to the First Canadian Army as staff liaison officer.

He moved with the regiment throughout France, Belgium, Holland and Germany.

In 1945 he was discharged from active duty and for his services was mentioned in dispatches and

decorated by Britain as a Member of the Order of the British Empire and by the Netherland's government as an officer of the Order of Orange Nassau with swords.

On his return to Canada he rejoined the SD and G Highlanders reserve battalion and commanded the regiment as lieutenant colonel until he retired in 1953.

He was awarded the Canadian Forces Decoration.

The former service man is survived by his wife, Mona McMaster and his children, Mrs. Philip J. Webb (Mona Lou), Don Mills, Ont.; David Marshal Irvine, Smith's Cove, N.S.; John Marshall Irvine, Cornwall; and Douglas Marshall Irvine at home.

Also surviving is one brother Lawrence Craibe Irvine of St. Lambert, Que.

He was also active in community affairs.

He was a member of Knox United Church and served as chairman of the trustees board of managers and sessions.

Mr. Irvine was first president and founder of the Cornwall branch of the Canadian Cancer Society, member of Red Cross Society and Canadian Legion Branch 297 and a life member of SD and G Highlanders officer's mess and the Corporation of Cornwall General Hospital.

Honorary pallbearers will be Philip D. Magor, Robert F. Gray, Neil P. McGillis, Col. J. W. Franklin, J. D. MacPhail, and Dr. George H. Tomlinson.

A Loss To The Community *Sat Dec 19 1970*

Cornwall lost a well-known citizen last week when A. Marshall Irvine died after a lengthy illness. Citizens paid tribute to his memory at a memorial service this week and no tribute was greater deserved for Marshall Irvine was a fine, sincere, community-minded citizen, highly respected as a gentleman, for his business integrity, and also for his distinguished military career.

A retired employee of Howard Smith Paper Mills, Ltd., and subsequently the Domtar organization, Mr. Irvine came to Cornwall in 1933. In 1963 he was transferred to Senneville, Que., where he was administrator of the Domtar research plant until his retirement in 1969. At that time he returned to Cornwall where he had resided until his death.

Mr. Irvine was a popular member of the S, D and G Highlanders. He enlisted in the reserve unit in 1938, and went into active duty with the Regiment in August, 1939. He served overseas in various capacities and his illustrious career brought him mention in dispatches. He was awarded the Member of the Order of the British Empire by Britain, and the Netherlands government honoured him with an officer of the Order of Orange Nassau with swords award. He was discharged from the army in 1945 as a Major. He remained active with the S, D and G Highlanders reserve battalion and served as Lieutenant-Colonel of the Unit.

A native of St. John, N.B., Marshall Irvine contributed much to the community life of Cornwall during his residence in the city. He was one of Cornwall's finest gentlemen and his death is a great loss to his family and the community. This newspaper joins the citizens of Cornwall in expressing sincerest sympathy to Mrs. Irvine and family.

116

18. Detailed Family Charts for 4th to 7th Generation

Descendants of Alexander (Sandy) IRVINE

Alexander (Sandy) IRVINE (b. 1841-Saint John, New Brunswick d. 12 Sep 1911-Granville Ferry, Annapolis Co., NS, Canada)

  sp: Mary E. PIGGOTT (b. Jun 1847-Nova Scotia, Canada m. 1864 d. 27 Nov 1919-Granville Ferry, N.S)

    └─ Lillian IRVINE (b. Sep 1865-Granville Ferry, Nova Scotia d. 1924 (Approx.))

        sp: Frank B / MORGAN (b. Abt 1862-Nova Scotia m. 4 Nov 1893)

        ├─ Frank Wishard / MORGAN (b. 1874 d. 4 Mar 1874-Derbyshire, Yorkshire - West Riding, United Kingdom)

        ├─ Eva Estelle / MORGAN (b. 12 Mar 1876-Granville Ferry d. 7 Oct 1957)

            sp: Alfred William Dr. PETT Dr. (b. 18 Aug 1869-Chelsea Christ Church, England d. 9 Apr 1933-Providence, Providence, RI, USA)

            ├─ Alexander Irvine Sr. PETT (b. 15 Apr 1907-Rhode Island d. 8 Jul 1980-Lehigh Acres, Lee, Florida, United States of America){+}

                sp: Rossette (Rose) Adeline NYLEN (b. 31 May 1909-Chicago, Cook Co., IL, USA d. 16 Mar 2005-Hopwood, F, Pennsylvania)

                ├─ Alexander Irvine PETT (b. 8 Aug 1932-Rhode Island, USA d. 10 Aug 1992-Illinois, USA)

                ├─ Richard PETT (b. Abt 1933-Rhode Island)

                ├─ Ann PETT (b. Abt 1935-Rhode Island)

                └─ Avis PETT (b. Abt 1937-Rhode Island)

            ├─ Harry G PETT (b. 10 May 1915-Rhode Island d. 13 Aug 1989-Grand Haven, Ottawa, Michigan){+}

                sp: Lois C L TANIS (b. 29 May 1917-Michigan d. 1 Apr 2005-Holland MI)

                ├─ Harry Gregory PETT, JR (b. 1 Oct 1942-New York, United States d. 9 Jul 1992-Cleveland, Cuyahoga, Ohio)

                └─ Mark E. PETT (b. 4 Apr 1945-Ohio, United States d. Feb 1988-Owings Mills, Baltimore, Maryland, USA)

            sp: Dr Alfred W PETT (b. 8 Aug 1871-Chelsea, Middlesex, England d. 9 Apr 1933-Providence, Providence, RI, United States)

            ├─ Alfred William Jr. PETT (b. 11 Apr 1906-Providence, Providence, Rhode Island, USA d. Jun 1975-, , United States of America){+}

                sp: Mary Irene BRIDGES (b. 29 Jul 1909-Gaffney, Cherokee, SC, United States d. 9 Aug 1992-Shelby, C, NC, United States)

            ├─ Alexander Irvine Sr. PETT (b. 15 Apr 1907-Rhode Island d. 8 Jul 1980-L, L, F, United States of America){+} ** Printed on Page 1 **

            └─ Harry G PETT (b. 10 May 1915-Rhode Island d. 13 Aug 1989-Grand Haven, Ottawa, Michigan){+} ** Printed on Page 1 **

        └─ Violet / MORGAN (b. 1880-Granville Ferry, Nova Scotia, Canada d. Oct 1945-Rutland, Vermont, USA)

    ├─ Frank Wishard IRVINE (b. 27 Aug 1874-Yarmouth, Nova Scotia d. 4 Mar 1954-New York, N.Y.)

        sp: Paulina SCHROEDER (b. Mar 1879-Omaha, Nebraska, USA m. 1903 d. 9 Oct 1956-Paramus, New Jersey, USA)

        ├─ Louise P. IRVINE (b. 3 Mar 1906-Kings, New York, USA d. 25 May 1906)

        ├─ John Alexander IRVINE (b. 9 Mar 1907-Woodcliff Lake, New Jersey, USA d. 6 Sep 1956)

        └─ Hope June IRVINE (b. 14 Jul 1910-New Jersey d. 27 May 1911)

    ├─ Eva Estelle / IRVINE (b. 12 Mar 1876-Yarmouth, Nova Scotia, Canada d. 7 Oct 1957-Providence, Providence, Rhode Island, USA)

        sp: Alfred William Dr. PETT Dr. (b. 18 Aug 1869-Chelsea Christ Church, England m. 11 Aug 1903 d. 9 Apr 1933-Providence, P, RI, USA)

        └─ Alfred William Jr. PETT (b. 11 Apr 1906-Providence, P, RI, USA d. Jun 1975-W, , , United States of America){+} ** Printed on Page 1 **

    └─ Violet Ethel IRVINE (b. Mar 1878-Granville Ferry, Nova Scotia d. 20 Dec 1945-Rutland, Vermont, USA)

        sp: Charles Albert TUTTLE (b. 12 Jan 1886-Framingham Massachusetts USA m. Mar 1909 d. 23 Jan 1952-Rutland, Vermont)

        ├─ Eva M TUTTLE (b. 23 Oct 1910-Dorchester, Massachusetts, USA d. 15 Oct 1998-Burlington, Vermont, USA)

        └─ Charles Albert Jr. TUTTLE (b. 19 Jun 1918-Vermont d. May 1973-Stoddard New Hampshire USA)

            sp: Bessie (b. Abt 1914-Oklahoma d. Texas)

Descendants of Hugh Marshall IRVINE

Hugh Marshall IRVINE (b. 6 Nov 1843-Saint John, N.B. d. 12 Jul 1913-Granville Ferry, NS)

sp: Martha Ann MILLS (b. 6 Nov 1843-Granville Ferry, N.S. m. 6 Nov 1867 d. 5 May 1922-Granville Ferry, N.S.)

— John Alfred IRVINE (b. 20 Sep 1868-Granville Ferry, Nova Scotia d. 18 Jul 1928-Red Deer, Alta.)

   sp: Mina Celia BUCKLEY (b. 20 Nov 1879-Halifax, N.S m. 12 Sep 1901 d. 19 May 1967-Calgary, AB)

    — Hugh Avery IRVINE (b. 10 Jun 1905-Halifax, N.S.)

      sp: Fern Edna LIDDLE (b. 26 Mar 1911-Rockford, Ill. USA m. 6 Oct 1934)

        — Bonnie Marleen IRVINE (b. 24 May 1936-Indian Head, Saskatchewan)

          sp: Kenneth William CURL (b. 16 Feb 1933-Panoka, Alberta m. 5 May 1956)

        — Noel Barrie IRVINE (b. 24 Dec 1937-Calgary, Alberta)

          sp: June Dorothy Anne BURGESS (b. 13 Mar 1940-Vancouver, B.C. m. 11 Nov 1961)

        — Tanga Delane Rose IRVINE (b. 28 Nov 1946-Victoria, B.C.)

          sp: Ronald Gregory LAMBERT (b. 26 Jan 1948-Victoria, B.C. m. 25 Jul 1970)

            └ Glen Robert LAMBERT (b. 15 Jul 1973-Victoria, B.C.)

        └ Victoria Stan-Lee IRVINE (b. 29 Dec 1950-Victoria, B.C.)

    — Inez Abigail IRVINE (b. 22 Aug 1907-Halifax, N.S.)

      sp: Edwin Wallace PRATER (b. 5 Dec 1908-Amity, Oregon, USA m. 23 Jan 1943)

    — William Douglas IRVINE (b. 6 Aug 1910-Calgary, Alberta d. 12 Apr 1972)

      sp: Ida Christina BRACKMAN (b. 11 Mar 1910-Calgary, Alberta m. 15 Jun 1935 d. 15 Mar 1981)

        — Carol Denise IRVINE (b. 24 Feb 1939-Edmonton, Alberta)

          sp: Samuel Friedrich LENTZ (b. 14 Jun 1938-Brightview, Alberta m. 27 Dec 1963)

        — Un-named IRVINE (b. 24 Feb 1939-Edmonton, Alberta d. 24 Feb 1939)

        └ Raymond Douglas IRVINE (b. 28 Jun 1950-Winnipeg, Manitoba)

    — Enid Eileen IRVINE (b. 12 Feb 1912-Calgary General Hosp, AB d. 1912-Calgary. AB)

    — John Alexander (Jack) IRVINE (b. 12 Apr 1913-Calgary, Alberta)

      sp: Florence Evelyn FLYNN (b. 1 Feb 1923-St. Albert, Alberta m. 25 Jul 1955)

        └ Wayne John IRVINE (b. 10 Sep 1958-Calgary, Alberta)

    └ Wilfred Harland IRVINE (b. 25 Jan 1918-Calgary, Alberta d. 26 Oct 1986-Victoria, B.C.)

      sp: Joyce Elinor STEWART (b. 20 Jan 1921-Lethbridge, Alberta m. 2 Jun 1951 d. 13 Aug 1999-Calgary, Alta.)

        — Harland Stewart IRVINE (b. 5 Sep 1952-St. Paul's Hospital, Vancouver, B.C.)

          sp: Dianne Elizabeth Nora FISHER (b. 17 Mar 1952-Red Deer, Alberta m. 4 May 1974)

            — Sarah Jane IRVINE (b. 28 Jul 1978-Kingston General Hospital, Kingston, Ontario)

            — Bronwyn Elizabeth IRVINE (b. 2 Dec 1981-Red Deer Hospital, Red Deer, Alberta)

            └ Brody John IRVINE (b. 9 Apr 1985-Foothills Hospital, Calgary, Alberta)

        └ David John IRVINE (b. 21 Feb 1956-Vancouver General Hospital, Vancouver, B.C.)

          sp: Mary Ann CALLISTER (b. 10 Feb 1959-Salt Lake City, Utah m. 31 Aug 1978(div))

            — Melissa Ann IRVINE (b. 3 May 1980-Provo General Hospital, Provo, Utah)

              sp: Ramsay Gutierrez BRYAN (b. 21 Oct 1977-Roy, Utah m. 12 Sep 2003)

          sp: Valerie Elaine MACMILLAN (b. 30 Aug 1954-Royal Alexandra Hospital, Edmonton, Alberta m. 3 Aug 1991)

            — Hayley Joy IRVINE (b. 17 Mar 1993-Foothills Hospital, Calgary, Alberta)

            └ Chandra Marie IRVINE (b. 29 Feb 1996-Foothills Hospital, Calgary, Alberta)

William IRVINE

John R IRVINE

Elizabeth IRVINE

Alton David IRVINE (b. 21 Nov 1874-Granville Ferry, Nova Scotia d. 1 Apr 1956-Vancouver, BC)

sp: Adeline Mary (Addie) ROBERTSON (b. 8 Jun 1882-Iroquois, Ontario m. 27 Dec 1904 d. 9 Aug 1966-North Vancouver, BC)

Doris Margaret IRVINE (b. 8 Jan 1910-Calgary, Alberta d. Mar 1980-Edmonton, Alberta)

sp: Leslie Neal HARRIS (b. 15 Sep 1905-Walthamstow, Essex, England m. 28 Sep 1934 d. 21 Sep 1971-Beaverlodge, Alberta)

Joan Margaret HARRIS (b. 25 Sep 1935-Grande Prairie, AB)

sp: David Ronald SEREDA (b. 26 Jun 1937-Edmonton, Alberta m. 11 Jun 1960 d. 19 Jul 2002-Edmonton, Alberta)

Sandra Jane SEREDA (b. 16 Oct 1963-Royal Alexandra Hospital, Edmonton, Alberta)

sp: Eugene Alan GOLDIE (b. 26 Aug 1965-Revelstoke, BC)

Leslie David SEREDA (b. 3 Apr 1975-Edmonton Gen. Hosp, Edmonton, AB)

sp: Anna Stephanie FERENC (b. 26 Dec 1978-Edmonton, AB m. 23 Aug 2003)

Jacqueline Mae SEREDA (b. 20 Feb 1999-Royal Alexandra Hospital, Edmonton, Alberta)

sp: Bradley John SCHIMPF (b. 15 Mar 1963-Edmonton, Alberta m. 27 Apr 1991)

Neal Alton HARRIS (b. 27 Dec 1937-Beaverlodge, Alberta)

sp: Jean Audrey JOHNSON (b. 25 Feb 1943-Camrose, AB m. 16 Jul 1966)

Florence Elizabeth IRVINE (b. 20 Dec 1914-Stavely, Alberta d. 23 Jul 2006-Parksville, BC)

sp: Truman Harry HARRISON (b. 4 Mar 1914-Lethbridge, Alberta m. 19 Aug 1939 d. 21 Jan 1989-Ganges, BC)

Delmar HARRISON (b. 2 Aug 1941-Medicine Hat, AB)

sp: Wendy Minerva FRIESEN (RUSSELL) (b. 1944 m. 12 Jan 1963(div) d. 7 Jan 2004-Vancouver, B.C.)

Kieran HARRISON (DIXON) (b. 29 Jul 1963-Vancouver, B.C.)

sp: Besi Nabatanzi BLASIO (b. 1947-Entebbe, Uganda m. 13 Oct 1971(div))

Roger HARRISON (b. 13 Aug 1969-Mwanza, Tanzania)

Diana Tina HARRISON (b. 9 May 1971-Entebbe, Uganda)

sp: Julita BALA SINDAC (b. 18 May 1947-Tayabas, Phillippines m. 19 Jul 1997)

Patricia Ann HARRISON (b. 31 Mar 1943-Medicine Hat, AB)

Descendants of John Edward IRVINE

John Edward IRVINE (b. 29 Dec 1846-Saint John, N.B. d. Mar 1911-44 Windsor Ave., Westmount, P.Q.)

sp: Julia Elvira WHITE (b. 28 Jan 1852-Springfield, New Brunswick m. 15 Oct 1874 d. 6 Apr 1938-Saint John, N.B.)

— Mary Edna IRVINE (b. 25 Dec 1875-Springfield, N.B. d. 13 Sep 1963-Saint John General Hospital, Saint John, N.B.)

   sp: James Edwin Clarke ANGEVINE (b. 10 Feb 1873-Saint John, N.B. m. 18 Sep 1900 d. 4 Jan 1936-Montreal, P.Q.)

     — John Blackburn (Jack) ANGEVINE (b. 10 Jun 1902-Saint John, N.B. d. Aft 1985-Bracebridge, Ontario)

       sp: Olive Brownell STANTON (b. 21 Feb 1903-Montreal, P.Q. m. 16 May 1931)

     — Daniel Murray ANGEVINE Dr. (b. 8 Oct 1903-Saint John, N.B. d. 8 Feb 1983-Madison, Dane, Wisconsin, United States of America)

       sp: Dorothy Edna SHEPPARD (b. 19 Aug 1907-P, , , United States of America m. 8 Jul 1933 d. 18 Oct 1998-, , , United States of Am)

        — James Murray ANGEVINE Dr. (b. 10 Dec 1934-New York, N.Y. d. 1977-Madison, Dane, Wisconsin, United States)

         sp: Marilou BUTLER (b. 4 Mar 1936-Madison, Wisc. m. 15 Jun 1957)

          — Douglas Reed ANGEVINE (b. 19 Jul 1960-Chicago, ILl d. Aft 2000-Plano, Texas)

          — Charles Daniel ANGEVINE (b. 17 Apr 1963-Chicago, ILl d. Aft 1977-Madison, WI)

            sp: Margaret Tracy STEWART (b. 1966 m. 23 May 1992)

          — Julie Michelle ANGEVINE (b. 17 Nov 1965-Denver, Colorado d. Aft 1977-Madison, WI)

        — Charles Douglas Dr. ANGEVINE Dr. (b. 9 Jul 1937-New York, N.Y. d. 1991-Fairport, Monroe, New York, United States)

         sp: Susan Jane GUNDERSON (b. 29 Aug 1937-Madison, Wisc. m. 25 Jun 1960)

          — Bruce Nathan / ANGEVINE (b. 11 Sep 1967-Phoenix, Ariz. d. Aft 1991-Fairport, Monroe co., NY)

            sp: Lynn Ann MCDANIEL (m. 23 Mar 2004)

          — Peter Douglas / ANGEVINE (b. 14 Jun 1970-Rochester, New York d. Aft 1991-Fairport, NY)

        — Judith Melanie / ANGEVINE (b. 8 Mar 1939-New York, United States d. 1977-Saratoga, Santa Clara, California, United States)

         sp: Eugene John FLATH (b. 13 Jul 1937-Green Bay, Wisc. m. 6 Jun 1961)

          — John Murray FLATH (b. 23 Dec 1962-Kittery, Maine)

          — Steven Christopher FLATH (b. 17 Nov 1964-Portsmouth, N.H.)

          — Peter William FLATH (b. 3 Oct 1966-Mountain View, Cal.)

          — Susan Ann FLATH (b. 23 Jun 1969-Palo Alto, Cal.)

     — Edwin Douglas ANGEVINE (b. 26 Jul 1905-Saint John, N.B. d. 6 Dec 1966-Saint John General Hosp., Saint John, N.B.)

       sp: Harriet Gwendolyne MACLEOD (b. Mar 1908-Winnipeg, Manitoba, Canada m. 16 Sep 1933)

        — David MacLeod ANGEVINE (b. 1 Jul 1937-Saint John, N.B.)

         sp: Elizabeth Jane KIERSTEAD (b. 13 Dec 1938-Saint John, N.B. m. 10 Sep 1960)

          — Heather Jane ANGEVINE (b. 3 Oct 1961-Saint John, N.B.)

          — David Douglas ANGEVINE (b. 11 Jan 1964-Saint John, N.B. d. Aft 1977-St John, New Brunswick){+}

        — Gerald Edwin ANGEVINE Ph.D (b. 25 Feb 1941-Saint John, N.B. d. Aft 1995-Calgary, Alberta)

         sp: Sherie Lee COBHAM (b. 26 Jun 1943-Saint John, N.B. m. 3 Jul 1965)

          — Jill Terilee ANGEVINE (b. 1 Apr 1968-Ottawa, Ont. d. Aft 1977-Toronto, Ontario, Canada)

          — Lauri Kate ANGEVINE (b. 10 Nov 1969-Ann Arbor, Mich. d. Aft 1977-Toronto, Canada)

            sp: Lyle Kendall GRANT (m. 5 Dec 2001)

          — Derek Michael ANGEVINE (b. 25 Sep 1972-Ottawa, Ont. d. Aft 1977-Toronto, Ontario, Canadfa)

          — Gregory Scott ANGEVINE (b. 30 Mar 1979)

        — Mary Louise ANGEVINE (b. 30 Jan 1945-Saint John, N.B. d. 15 Mar 1945-Saint John, N.B.)

     — James Stuart ANGEVINE (b. 7 Jan 1909-Hampton, Kings, New Brunswick, Canada d. 10 May 1992-Brantford, Ontario, Canada)

       sp: Margaret Eleanor LOGAN (b. 28 Mar 1912-Saint John, N.B. m. 31 Aug 1935)

        — John Stuart ANGEVINE (b. 29 Aug 1937-Saint John, N.B. d. Aft 1977-Toronto, Ontario)

        — Hugh Gordon ANGEVINE (b. 8 Feb 1941-Saint John, N.B. d. Aft 1998-Brantford, Ontario)

        — Donald Frederick ANGEVINE (b. 24 Jul 1945-Saint John, N.B. d. Aft 1977-Brantford, Ontario)

sp: UNKNOWN

  └─ James Eric ANGEVINE (b. 22 May 1976-Guelph, Ontario d. Aft 1977-Brantford, Ontario, Canada)

└─ Robert Walter ANGEVINE (b. 7 Sep 1951-St. John, New Brunswick d. Aft 1995-Edmonton, Alberta, Canada)

── William Henry (Harry) IRVINE (b. 25 Feb 1878-Saint John, N.B. d. 15 Nov 1957-Toronto, Ont.)

 sp: Martha UNKNOWN (b. Jun 1873-England)

 sp: Ada Mary BRYANT (b. Jun 1873-Malvern, Worchestershire, England)

  ── Walter William IRVINE (b. Abt 1905-Toronto, York, Ontario, Canada d. Bef 1911-Toronto, York, Ontario, Canada)

  ── Kenneth Bryant IRVINE (b. Abt 1907-Toronto, York, Ontario, Canada d. Bef 1911-Toronto, York, Ontario, Canada)

  ── Henry Erskine Bryant IRVINE Sir (b. 25 Jul 1909-Toronto, York, Ontario, Canada d. May 1992-Lewes, Sussex, England)

   sp: Valborg Cecilie CARSLUND (b. 14 Apr 1904-Fyn, Denmark m. 4 Feb 1945 d. Feb 1990-Great Ote Hall, BH, Lewes, Sussex, UK)

    ── Carola GODMAN-IRVINE

     sp: Victor Richard LAW (b. 21 Oct 1941-Edinburgh, UK m. 10 Jun 1982)

      ── Matthew Frederic Harry Godman LAW (b. 12 Apr 1983-London, UK)

      ── Charley Victor Colton LAW (b. 6 Dec 1984-London, UK)

      ── Catrina (Nina) Clare LAW (b. 4 Sep 1987-Westminster, Greater London)

    └─ Jaqueline (Jaci) GODMAN-IRVINE (b. 26 Jun 1948)

     sp: Michael HARMAN (m. 28 Nov 1981(div))

      ── Tamarind Valborg HARMAN (b. 15 Nov 1982)

      ── Thorin Bryant HARMAN (b. 26 Aug 1984)

  ── Judith Elvira Ada Bryant IRVINE (b. 25 Jan 1912-Toronto, Ont. d. 23 Mar 1932-Wandsworth, Greater London, England)

── Arthur Marshall IRVINE Sr. (b. 12 Jul 1881-Saint John, New Brunswick d. 14 Aug 1952-Cornwall General Hosp., Cornwall, Ontario)

 sp: Lulah Louise CRAIBE (b. 14 Nov 1881-Sussex, New Brunswick m. 3 Jun 1905 d. 27 Oct 1957-Royal Victoria Hosp., Montreal, Quebec)

  ── Arthur Marshall IRVINE Lt-Col. (b. 15 Mar 1906-Saint John, New Brunswick d. 11 Dec 1970-Cornwall, Ontario)

   sp: Margaret Mona MCMASTER (b. 1 Apr 1908-Westmount, Quebec m. 1931 d. 25 Feb 1999-Sandfield Place, Cornwall, Ont.)

    ── Mona Louise IRVINE (b. 22 Feb 1933-Montreal, P.Q.)

     sp: Philip John WEBB (b. 2 Jul 1930-Grace Hospital, Toronto, Ontario m. 6 Aug 1960 d. 5 May 2010-Toronto ontario cananda)

      ── Philip Marshall WEBB (b. 24 Mar 1962-Toronto East General Hosp., Toronto, Ontario)

      ── Peter Livingstone WEBB (b. 29 Apr 1966-Toronto Western General Hosp., Toronto, Ontario)

       sp: Kristen Lee DUFFY (b. 27 Mar 1966-Woburn, Mass. m. 27 Oct 1990(div))

       sp: Denise I. GARCIA (b. 18 Sep 1969-San Francisco, CA m. 15 Dec 2007)

      ── Andrea Lynne WEBB (b. 12 Dec 1969-Toronto Western General Hosp., Toronto, Ontario)

       sp: Bradley Alexander MACDONELL (m. 28 Oct 2000)

    ── David Marshall IRVINE (b. 11 Nov 1935-Cornwall, Ontario)

     sp: Sylvia Jean SMITH (b. 24 Sep 1938-Cornwall, Ontario m. 10 Feb 1962)

      ── Geoffrey DePoint IRVINE (b. 7 Jul 1965-Lakeshore General Hosp., Pointe Claire, Quebec)

       sp: Kelly Lynn MACDONALD (b. 21 Jul 1966-Peterborough, Ontario m. 20 Jul 1991)

      ── Jennifer Roop IRVINE (b. 22 Jul 1970-Digby, Nova Scotia)

       sp: Robert Edward BEGRAND (b. 2 May 1970-Wakaw, Saskatchewan m. 23 Jul 1994)

    ── John Marshall IRVINE (b. 3 Jul 1944-Cornwall General Hospital, Cornwall, Ontario)

     sp: Mary Heather DEWAR (b. 11 Nov 1943 m. 8 Jun 1973(div))

      ── James Andrew McMaster IRVINE (b. 11 Apr 1978-Hotel Dieu Hosp., Cornwall, Ontario)

       sp: Sonja LOCKYER (b. 7 Sep 1979 m. 22 Jun 2012)

      ── Jonathan Edward Marshall IRVINE (b. 10 Feb 1980-Hotel Dieu Hospital, Cornwall, Ontario)

     sp: Gloria Elizabeth NAPP (b. 2 Feb 1951-Lachute, Quebec m. 26 Jun 1999)

121

Descendants of John Edward IRVINE

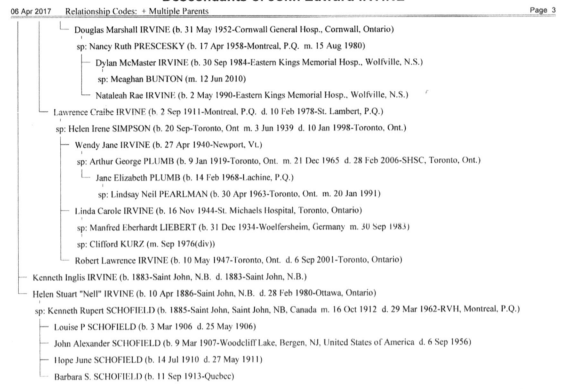

Douglas Marshall IRVINE (b. 31 May 1952-Cornwall General Hosp., Cornwall, Ontario)

  sp: Nancy Ruth PRESCESKY (b. 17 Apr 1958-Montreal, P.Q. m. 15 Aug 1980)

    Dylan McMaster IRVINE (b. 30 Sep 1984-Eastern Kings Memorial Hosp., Wolfville, N.S.)

      sp: Meaghan BUNTON (m. 12 Jun 2010)

    Nataleah Rae IRVINE (b. 2 May 1990-Eastern Kings Memorial Hosp., Wolfville, N.S.)

Lawrence Craibe IRVINE (b. 2 Sep 1911-Montreal, P.Q. d. 10 Feb 1978-St. Lambert, P.Q.)

  sp: Helen Irene SIMPSON (b. 20 Sep-Toronto, Ont m. 3 Jun 1939 d. 10 Jan 1998-Toronto, Ont.)

    Wendy Jane IRVINE (b. 27 Apr 1940-Newport, Vt.)

      sp: Arthur George PLUMB (b. 9 Jan 1919-Toronto, Ont. m. 21 Dec 1965 d. 28 Feb 2006-SHSC, Toronto, Ont.)

        Jane Elizabeth PLUMB (b. 14 Feb 1968-Lachine, P.Q.)

          sp: Lindsay Neil PEARLMAN (b. 30 Apr 1963-Toronto, Ont. m. 20 Jan 1991)

    Linda Carole IRVINE (b. 16 Nov 1944-St. Michaels Hospital, Toronto, Ontario)

      sp: Manfred Eberhardt LIEBERT (b. 31 Dec 1934-Woelfersheim, Germany m. 30 Sep 1983)

      sp: Clifford KURZ (m. Sep 1976(div))

    Robert Lawrence IRVINE (b. 10 May 1947-Toronto, Ont. d. 6 Sep 2001-Toronto, Ontario)

Kenneth Inglis IRVINE (b. 1883-Saint John, N.B. d. 1883-Saint John, N.B.)

Helen Stuart "Nell" IRVINE (b. 10 Apr 1886-Saint John, N.B. d. 28 Feb 1980-Ottawa, Ontario)

  sp: Kenneth Rupert SCHOFIELD (b. 1885-Saint John, Saint John, NB, Canada m. 16 Oct 1912 d. 29 Mar 1962-RVH, Montreal, P.Q.)

    Louise P SCHOFIELD (b. 3 Mar 1906 d. 25 May 1906)

    John Alexander SCHOFIELD (b. 9 Mar 1907-Woodcliff Lake, Bergen, NJ, United States of America d. 6 Sep 1956)

    Hope June SCHOFIELD (b. 14 Jul 1910 d. 27 May 1911)

    Barbara S. SCHOFIELD (b. 11 Sep 1913-Quebec)

Made in the USA
Lexington, KY
24 October 2017